American

Bloomsbury

Louisa May Alcott,

Ralph Waldo Emerson, Margaret Fuller,

Nathaniel Hawthorne, and

Henry David Thoreau: Their Lives, Their

Loves, Their Work

SUSAN CHEEVER

SIMON & SCHUSTER

New York   London   Toronto   Sydney

SIMON & SCHUSTER
Rockefeller Center
1230 Avenue of the Americas
New York, NY 10020

SIMON & SCHUSTER and colophon are registered trademarks
of Simon & Schuster, Inc.

For information about special discounts for bulk purchases,
please contact Simon & Schuster Special Sales at
1-800-456-6798 or business@simonandschuster.com.

Designed by Dana Sloan

Manufactured in the United States of America

1 3 5 7 9 10 8 6 4 2

Library of Congress Cataloging-in-Publication Data
Cheever, Susan.
American Bloomsbury : Louisa May Alcott, Ralph Waldo Emerson, Margaret Fuller,
Nathaniel Hawthorne, and Henry David Thoreau : their lives, their loves,
their work / Susan Cheever.
        p.   cm.
Includes bibliographic references and index.
1. Authors, American—Homes and haunts—Massachusetts—Concord.
2. American literature—Massachusetts—Concord—History and criticism.
3. Authors, American—19th century—Biography. 4. Concord (Mass.)—Intellectual
life—19th century. 5. Concord (Mass.)—Biography. I. Title.
PS255.C6C48   2006
810.9'97444—dc22   2006045015
ISBN-13: 978-0-7432-6461-7
ISBN-10: 0-7432-6461-4

Photo Credits
Berkshire Athenaeum: 16; Concord Free Public Library: 1, 2, 3, 4, 5, 6, 8, 9, 10, 15;
Quad Hinckle: 11; National Portrait Gallery, Smithsonian Institution/Art Resource,
NY: 13; Orchard House/The L. M. Alcott Memorial Association: 7, 12; Peabody
Essex Museum: 14; The Pierpont Morgan Library/Art Resource: title page.

CONTENTS

———◆———

For my children, who shared in this great adventure.

I think we escape something by living in the villages. In Concord here there is some milk of life, we are not so raving distracted with wind and dyspepsia. The mania takes a milder form. People go a-fishing, and know the taste of their meat. They cut their own whippletree in the woodlot, they know something practically of the sun and the east wind, of the underpinning and the roofing of the house, of the pan and mixture of the soils.

—Journals of Ralph Waldo Emerson

There is always room and occasion enough for a true book on any subject, as there is room for more light on the brightest day, and more rays will not interfere with the first.

—The Journal of Henry David Thoreau

A NOTE TO THE READER

This book follows the lives of five principal characters and dozens of their friends and family members over a period of about twenty-five years from 1840 to 1868. A few final scenes take place in the 1870s and 1880s.

I have tried to find a structure that follows the story chronologically and which also gives each character a chance to experience almost every event in the narrative. The result is a series of overlapping scenes in which some incidents are repeated, sometimes more than once. An important turning point will be seen through Hawthorne's eyes and then through Emerson's or Louisa May Alcott's before it is finally completely described. Each section of two to three chapters focuses on one character, and each character is at the center of the narrative four times during the book.

By this method I have tried to honor the characters, their lives, and their intimate connections with each other.

PREFACE

———◆———

In January 2000, my agent was asked to find a writer for an introduction to a new edition of *Little Women;* by chance I happened to call her about something else a few minutes later. She asked if I would like to do it. Sure, I said. I thought of *Little Women* as one of those books I had read a long time ago that was excellent back then. It was a book that elicited a sigh of recognition from me when it came up in conversation, but which I actually did not remember very clearly. I had seen the movie. I knew very little about Louisa May Alcott, although I had faded memories of a dreary, obligatory childhood visit to the Alcott House in Concord, Massachusetts.

The book amazed me. Far from being the string of bromides I dimly recalled, it was an elegantly written family story of great poignance and skill. Alcott's voice reached out through the century and a half since she had written, creating suspense even when I knew what was going to happen, drawing characters that seemed to come alive on the page, writing scenes of a texture and sensual detail that made them seem more real than the room where I read. Her prose style, clear and slightly, gently ironic, captivated me. I began to read about her, racing through Martha Saxton's and Madeleine Stern's biographies. The woman was even more interesting than her writing.

I was delighted to discover that Laurie, the boy next door in *Little Women,* was probably based on Henry David Thoreau, on whom Louisa had a crush, or was it Ralph Waldo Emerson, who actually lived next door to the Alcotts? The March girls' beloved absent father was Bronson Alcott, one of the founders of alternative education. The book I had vaguely loved as a girl reading about girls was actually a rich portrait of American writers at a specific moment in history.

Soon, I was immersed in reading about the group of men and women who came to be called Transcendentalists, discovering more and more coincidences of greatness being the result of proximity to greatness. I remembered F. O. Matthiessen's bold statement that all of American literature had been written between 1850 and 1855. What I hadn't realized is that most of it was written in the same cluster of three houses.

I wrote my introduction to *Little Women* and kept on writing.

Part One

1

CONCORD, MASSACHUSETTS

———◆———

The crossroads where the swampy meadows below the Cambridge Turnpike rise steeply to the orchards on the other side of the Lexington Road looks like any New England corner; shaded by maples, it is bordered by lush grass in the summer and piles of plowed snow in the winter. On the high side, two clapboard houses sit near the road. Across from them, a white house with a columned entrance is surrounded by lawns. It's the kind of house an ordinary merchant might have owned in the nineteenth century, but this intersection is an extraordinary place.

At various times, these three houses were home to Ralph Waldo Emerson and his family, Henry David Thoreau, Bronson Alcott and his daughter Louisa May, Nathaniel Hawthorne, and Margaret Fuller. Their neighbors were Henry James and his father, Emily Dickinson and Oliver Wendell Holmes, Henry Wadsworth Longfellow and Horace Mann. Their friends were Walt Whitman, Herman Melville, Henry Ward Beecher, and Edgar Allan Poe. From their collaborations with each other and the Concord landscape came almost every nineteenth-century American masterpiece—*Walden, The Scarlet Letter, Moby-Dick,* and *Little Women,* to name a few—as well as the ideas about men and women, nature, education, marriage, and writing that shape our world today.

We may think of them as static daguerreotypes, but in fact these men and women fell desperately in and out of love with each other, tormented each other in a series of passionate romantic triangles, edited each other's work, talked about ideas all night, and walked arm in arm under Concord's great elms. They picked apples together in the autumn, struggled with horses and carts through the spring mud, and swam in the Concord River in the summer. They mourned together when the Emersons lost their nine-year-old son, and rejoiced together when Anna Alcott married John Pratt.

They campaigned together for temperance and for abolition, subjects that were explored in lectures they gave at the local Lyceum, named after Aristotle's school outside of Athens, just one of the ways in which they expressed their admiration for Ancient Greece. They championed Greek Revival architecture, they studied and read Greek, and they adorned their living rooms and studies with busts of Plato and Socrates.

They bought and sold from each other, sometimes driving a hard bargain and sometimes failing to distinguish between a gift and a purchase. Thoreau talked Hawthorne into buying his handmade boat, the *Musketaquid*. The Alcotts sold the Hawthornes their house, an old pig farm fixed up by Bronson Alcott, and they moved into the wreck next door. As usual, Emerson gave them a loan. When Hawthorne babysat his five-year-old son Julian while his wife went to visit her sister, Herman Melville dropped by to help.

Louisa May Alcott was in love with Thoreau, who serenaded her on his flute, and then with Emerson. This Yankee Plato lent her books about sexy young girls and their older teachers that had been translated from the German by his good friend Margaret Fuller. Emerson, in turn, exchanged love letters with Margaret Fuller while she was staying as a guest in his house. Fuller died in a shipwreck in the waters off Fire Island, New York, which is described in a Louisa May Alcott novel. The novel, titled *Moods*, is about a young woman named Sylvia who falls in love simultaneously with an Emerson-like intellectual and a man at home in nature like Thoreau. When this novel was published, it got a bad review from Henry James. James later appropriated the adorable, defiant character of Jo March in Louisa May Alcott's *Little Women* as a model for his headstrong and independent American woman, Isabel Archer, in *Portrait of a Lady*.

When Emerson went to Europe, he left Thoreau in charge of his household with his wife and children. On his return, the house seemed too small. Thoreau borrowed a piece of Emerson's land on Walden

Pond and built his own place. They all loved Concord. Hawthorne called it Eden. Emerson wrote that he spent his best days there. Her Concord days were "the happiest of my life," Louisa May Alcott said. "Concord," wrote Henry James, is "the biggest little place in America."

What was it about the time and place—the mid nineteenth century in a landlocked town west of Boston—that caused this sudden outbreak of genius? Was it a political climate so heated that 80 percent of the electorate turned out to vote? Was it that most of these people drank little, ate a scant vegetarian diet, and were always terribly worried about money? Was it their devotion to family? Or was it just something in the air?

The town, with its center located just above the junction where the Sudbury and the Assabet rivers join to make the Concord River, had been settled since 1635. A community of farms and pastures, it numbered about 2,000 residents. Many Concord residents were the proud descendants of the men who had fired what Emerson called "the shot heard round the world," the shot that began the American Revolution on April 19, 1775.

Since Ancient Rome, theories have been offered to explain why geniuses seem to be grouped together in specific times and locations. The philosopher Velleius, writing about Plato, Aristotle, Aeschylus, Aristophanes, Euripides, and Sophocles, speculated that geniuses inspired envy, which attracted younger men in two ways: they came for inspiration, and they came in the hope of equaling and surpassing those who would teach them. Modern research on genius clusters has shown that circumstances, political conditions, landscape, and community forces sometimes come together to create an unusual concentration of talent. "Genius clusters may not be random as genius may attract genius," wrote Dr. William Foege in discussing another cluster, our founding fathers: Washington, Madison, Jefferson, and Franklin.

If those men were the fathers of our politics, the men and women of Concord were certainly the mothers and fathers of our literature. They formed the first American literary community. They defined our modern beliefs about environmentalism and conservation, and they praised the glorious importance of the individual self. They believed in feelings. "The Unitarians had pronounced human nature to be excellent," wrote Paul Brooks in *The People of Concord;* "the Transcendentalists pronounced it divine." They were this country's first professional authors, and they created a new kind of nonfiction memoir and a new kind of novel in which women and the details of domesticity have a central importance.

They lived and worked with a standard of living almost unimaginable to those of us who have grown up in the twentieth century. By all measures, standards of living stayed more or less the same for hundreds of years until the early 1900s, when they roared forward toward the comforts and opportunities we now take for granted. A world without electricity or effective medicine or dentistry, a world in which infant mortality was normal and most people did not live into middle age, a world without birth control, vaccinations, or central heating, air conditioning, and telephones, was a place where time took on a different quality than it has now. These people were closer to nature than we can ever be, of necessity—and they depended on friends and neighbors because they had to.

Physical discomfort may have added to their idealism—an idealism so ardent that it cast a shadow on good sense. They were high-minded intellectuals, men and women who—for the most part—lived according to principles that transcended things like warmth in the winter and regular dinners. But their fierceness on behalf of the causes they believed in ended by compromising their own ideals. As the Civil War approached, they were confused and divided. Their high-mindedness became self-righteousness, and they were seduced by the false authority of John Brown and others like him. Their innocence betrayed them.

This story begins in 1840 with the arrival of the Alcotts in Concord. Its chapters follow the lives of Louisa May Alcott, Emerson and Thoreau, Hawthorne and Margaret Fuller. The story will tell how Louisa May Alcott, ill and in a rage, sat down to write the book for girls that would be one of the best-selling novels of all time in 1868, and ends in 1882 with the death of Ralph Waldo Emerson. But this is not only a story about ideas and their power to form a national identity; it's about love triangles and the difficulties of raising children, about grief and inspiration and bad advice and passionate friendships, about the ebb and flow of daily life and the New England seasons in a small town.

2

THE ALCOTTS ARRIVE FOR
THE FIRST TIME

—◆—

If human nature was amenable to teaching, Louisa May Alcott would have been the perfect daughter. Her father, Bronson Alcott, believed that with the right kind of direction children could be brought into a state of peaceful harmony—as long as that direction came from a high-minded thinker like himself. It was in pursuit of this kind of perfection that Bronson Alcott decided to bring his family to live in Concord, Massachusetts, where he could find intellectual companionship in general, and the admiration of Ralph Waldo Emerson in particular—that and the fact that Emerson had offered to pay the rent.

The horse-drawn stage rumbled into Concord down the turnpike from Boston at the end of a spring afternoon in 1840. The wooden cab with a family inside and bags tied onto the top was pulled into town past Walden Pond and the marshes around it, and then past the First Parish Church and through Monument Square by an exhausted team of horses. After the more than three-hour trip, the stage drew up in front of the long porch of the Middlesex Hotel. The driver tied the reins to a hitching post under a huge elm. The family that climbed down, stretched, and looked around at their new surroundings was unusual even for a New England town in the 1840s.

The father was a tall man with a sweep of blond hair and a pronounced aquiline nose under the shade of a broad-brimmed tan-colored hat. Dressed simply in worn black clothing, and swinging a gleaming walking stick, he carried himself as if he was used to being listened to, and he stooped to hear the questions his three chattering daughters asked as if he were a great teacher and they his willing students. This was Bronson Alcott, the founder of the Temple School in Boston, which had recently caused a series of local scandals and finally gone bankrupt.

Alcott's "Conversations" in Boston, public forums in which he lectured and answered questions on subjects such as "Human Culture," "Man," and "Character" had attracted Emerson, who assured Alcott that in Concord he would find men with interests like his own, and a serious audience for his lectures. Emerson loved and supported Alcott, whose impractical, boyish presence always cheered him up. "I must think very ill of my age and country, if they cannot discover his extraordinary soul," he wrote. He had written furious letters in Alcott's defense when the press had attacked his writing, and he ascribed the loss of the Temple School to the stupidity of modern culture. Boston was a city in a kind of intellectual fever, Emerson believed. It was in the quieter precincts of Concord, calmed by the rhythms of village life, that men could think important thoughts uninterrupted by others' opinions and obligations.

Emerson would soon lure Nathaniel Hawthorne away from the nearby experimental Utopian community of Brook Farm in Roxbury and help install Hawthorne and his new wife Sophia Peabody in another Emerson house, the Old Manse on the other side of town near the Old North Bridge over the Concord River. That house, built by Emerson's grandfather William, had been lived in for almost sixty years by the Reverend Ezra Ripley, who died in 1839, leaving ownership of the house to his son Samuel, a minister in Waltham. Emerson had often stayed there, and he had written his famous essay *Nature* in its upstairs study. To welcome the newlyweds, Emerson would send his friend Henry David Thoreau to plant a flower and vegetable garden so that it would be flourishing on their arrival.

In the meantime, Emerson was entertaining Sophia Peabody—not yet married to Hawthorne—whose sister Elizabeth's bookshop on West Street in Boston had become a center of intellectual buzz. Sophia, who was an accomplished artist, had done a bas-relief of Emerson's beloved brother Charles, who had died in 1836. After that, Emerson had invited her to stay with his family in Concord. When Sophia had written that she looked forward to long conversations with Emerson when she moved to Concord, he had written back keeping her at a distance and instead offering up Bronson Alcott. "Mr. Alcott, the prince of conversers, lives little more than a mile from our house, and we will call on his aid as we often do," he wrote.

Lizzie Peabody's bookshop was also the setting for Margaret Fuller's first "Conversations," set up by Fuller with the intention of compensating for the lack of education for women in a world where they were not admitted to college, not allowed to vote, and not often permitted to own property. Fuller's first series on Greek mythology, including discussions of Prometheus, Bacchus, and Venus as the "paradigm of instinctive womanhood," had been a huge success. She planned a second series, on the fine arts. Margaret Fuller was also in the midst of publishing the first issue of *The Dial,* a magazine with lilac covers that would become the mouthpiece for Emerson and his friends for its two years of existence.

Emerson and Alcott, Fuller and their neighbor Henry David Thoreau, who lived in town with his family, were all part of a movement that was beginning to be called Transcendentalism. Transcendentalism officially began with meetings organized by Frederic Henry Hedge, whose father was a Harvard professor and whose essay on Coleridge had delighted Emerson.

Hedge, a minister, had moved to Bangor, Maine, but he missed Concord. To keep himself in touch with his old community, he organized a series of meetings beginning in 1836 in Cambridge. Hedge's Club, as it was originally called, included James Freeman Clarke, Emerson, and Bronson Alcott among others and was later joined by Thoreau, Theodore Parker, Margaret Fuller, and Elizabeth Peabody. The Transcendentalists who met in Hedge's Club were the original hippies—young, smart, and dedicated to the overthrow of the stuffy existing authorities.

These authorities included the old Calvinism of the Puritans and the practical humanism of New England Unitarianism. Transcendentalism deified nature and dealt in the kinds of marvels and wonders that sometimes even transcended things like having enough to eat or making a living. It replaced the literalness of Locke with the moral imperatives of Kant. "A wonderless age is Godless," Alcott had written with his typical contempt for clarity. He sometimes called Transcendentalism "the newness." Alcott embraced the idea of Concord, which he insisted on calling Concordia.

The Concord group of Transcendentalists was part of a wave of liberalism and a passion for freedom that seemed to be sweeping through the new United States. After decades of Puritan striving and dour farmers rising at dawn to tend to the necessities of crops and barns, after new governments creating hierarchies of necessary rules and regulatory structures, the battle for survival had been won.

The wilderness had once been a dangerous place that had to be tamed; now nature was a friendly environment to be enjoyed. The world was shifting. It was time to kick up our heels. In many ways, the period of the late 1830s and '40s was a time like the 1960s when individual adventure was prized and all the old rules suddenly seemed corrupt. "The new mood spread like the flowers of May," Van Wyck Brooks has written in his account of this in *The Flowering of New England.* "One heard the flute in the fields. Farmers and village tailors stopped to watch the birds building their nests. They went on woodland walks. They recorded the days when the wildflowers opened. They observed the little tragedies of nature that no one had noticed before. . . . They gathered the first hepaticas, the trailing arbutus that had bled unseen under the boots of their fathers."

Even the dour, handsome Nathaniel Hawthorne was not immune to this exuberant mood. "I want my place, my own place, my true place in the world," he wrote; "I want my proper sphere, my thing."

Suddenly, poetry, once a frivolous conceit, took center stage with its literary importance. Houses once built as simply as possible against the elements bloomed with the porticoes and columns of Greek Revival. In many villages, groups assembled in awe to watch the night-blooming cereus—a nocturnal flower recently imported from Mexico—slowly open its magical, languid petals.

The new energy generated by the escape from the Puritan dicta and the hard facts of New England life encouraged a reaching abroad for ideas and writing unprecedented in this country. Germany, as well as Greece, was raided by Emerson and his colleagues for new and exciting ideas. The great Thomas Carlyle, a Scottish writer living in London, was as much an inspiration as if he had been living in nearby Lexington.

Enchanted by Carlyle and his orphic questions—"Did the upholsterers make this universe? Were you created by the tailor?"—the new generation of Concord intellectuals was intoxicated with freedom, with leisure, and with the possibilities of a life devoted to thought and pleasure. In rejecting Unitarianism, the Transcendentalists were also trying to introduce a revolutionary new populism into the already hierarchical American democratic system. Emerson in particular hoped to help overthrow the existing intellectual elite, as represented by the Harvard community, and open the doors of American thought to anyone who had the largeness of heart and intellect required. "Man has encumbered himself with aged errors," Emerson wrote, "with usages and ceremonies, with law, property, church, customs, and books until he is almost smothered under his own institutions."

Influenced by Immanuel Kant's *Critique of Pure Reason,* Emerson, Thoreau, Alcott, and their followers believed in the power of intuition. They thought every man and even some women harbored a divine spark—every man including the poor and the rich, the hermit and the railroad worker and the landowner. They called this divine spark "reason." Sometimes this was an inner light; sometimes it was the voice of God. For others it was more direct—Thoreau's friend Jones Very thought that he himself was the new Messiah. "The all is in each particle," Emerson wrote. In a lecture in 1842, he explained Kant's belief that "there was a very important class of ideas, or imperative forms, which did not come by experience, but through which experience was acquired: that these were intuitions of the mind itself; and he denominated them Transcendental forms . . . whatever belongs to the class of intuitive thought is popularly called at the present day Transcendental."

All this new freedom didn't go unnoticed by the Old Guard. John Quincy Adams and Andrews Norton at Harvard agreed with their colleague Edward Everett, who found Emerson's fresh writing "conceited, laborious nonsense."

3

LOUISA, GIRL
INTERRUPTED

———◆———

Mrs. Bronson Alcott, who stepped down from the stage after her husband and children that spring afternoon, was an aristocratic woman whose fine bearing and light step had been worn down by life with a great man. In June, she would give birth to the Alcotts' fourth daughter. She wore an old-fashioned bonnet with a flaring wide brim, and a long muslin dress. As a young girl, Abigail May, known as Abba, had been the earnest daughter of a romantic, erratic father. Colonel Joseph May had won his rank in the Revolution. Abba's Boston upbringing had offered no attractive suitors, and she fell in love with Bronson Alcott, a visiting teacher, months before he returned her passion. At first, Alcott didn't seem to be the marrying kind. He had been a peddler before he was a teacher, and there was something about him that suggested the lightness of wandering, the ability to sleep on a stranger's floor or in the hay in an alien barn, and the quiet willingness to do without domestic comforts.

Nevertheless, after a long courtship, often veiled in plans for the education of the young or the relieving of the suffering of the poor, Abba and Bronson had been married in 1830 in a world where a woman's deference to her domestic duties and to her husband's wishes went unquestioned. Even the idea that women were more than possessions or able to think for themselves was heresy. There were already some rogue political voices questioning the morality of men owning slaves, but no one had yet thought to question the morality of men owning their wives. Although Bronson would dominate his family for a few more years, Abba Alcott already found herself making up for his deficiencies, always excused by high-mindedness, both in practical ways and with money borrowed from her family.

On that afternoon in 1840, she got down wearily from the stage with their three daughters—Anna, the eldest, whose behavior was the subject of some of her father's most positive essays on education; Lizzie, the youngest sister, whose sweetness had also captured her father's attention, and the eight-year-old Louy, or Louisa May, who had always been the rebel in the family, the least pretty sister, and the one whose energy and imagination sometimes seemed untamable. Bronson Alcott actually believed that a blond, blue-eyed complexion like his own went with a pureness of heart and goodness of soul, while dark hair and dark eyes often reflected an inner darkness.

Of the three sisters, Louisa was the dark one, and she had a "deep-seated obstinacy of temper," her father wrote in his long-winded and thorough *Observations on the Spiritual Nurture of My Children,* one of his many Transcendentalist tracts on the education of children. "She is still the undisciplined subject of her own instincts." At the time, she was one year old. This particular essay was written when the infant Louisa slapped the two-year-old Anna, leaving, as Bronson wrote with horror, "the mark of her sister's hand . . . on her cheek." As she grew older, Louisa was so boisterous that she believed she had been a horse in a previous life, a conviction that was not popular with her father. By the time she was ten, her role as the bad girl in the family was already set. "I have tried to be contented and I think I have been more so," she wrote to her mother in a mortified tone, nevertheless complaining about sharing a room with her sisters. "I have been thinking about my little room which I suppose I shall never have." She signed it "from your trying daughter, Louy."

Louisa's journals, kept daily, became a room of her own in a way—both her parents read them and commented on their contents. Naturally, in the journals Louisa is always failing and her parents are forgiving and utterly perfect. "Did my lessons, and in the P.M. mother read Kenilworth to us while we sewed," reads one typical entry. "It is splendid! I got angry and called Anna mean. Father told me to look out the word in the Dic., and it meant 'base', 'contemptible.' I was so ashamed to have called my dear sister that, and I cried over my bad tongue and temper." In a list of vices she wants to get rid of, Louisa lists idleness, willfulness, impudence, pride, and love of cats.

But it was springtime in Concord, the lilacs perfumed the air, and grapevines dripped from the broad white porches on Main Street, where a row of shops had been built along the Milldam, a bridge over the Mill Brook where it joined the Sudbury River. The apples were in bloom, and the slow curves of the river flowed between soft grassy banks spattered with jewelweed and purple loosestrife where willows leaned down to make delightful watery hiding places. In the woods under the pines, there were carpets of needles, striped with lichens and tiny red mushrooms. Hedges of berries lined the paths, and great shady elms stood in rows along the dirt streets. White picket fences bordered Main Street where the town's two main roads forked: one toward the Old North Bridge, where the colonial militia had halted the British redcoats on an April morning in 1775, and the other toward Boston. Concord, Massachusetts, was already at the center of American history. The first democratic constitution had been written by the Concord town fathers in the eighteenth century, and it was to Concord that Paul Revere was headed on his famous ride.

The next day, the Alcotts unpacked their trunks and settled into Dovecote Cottage, owned by Emerson's friends the Hosmer family, a long white house facing a picket fence with a gate that separated it from the road. The Alcott family began the day as their father deemed healthy with a breakfast of unleavened bread, water, and porridge. Poverty and Bronson Alcott's ideas about nutrition led the Alcotts to a severely restricted diet that included rice and graham meal, boiled squash and potatoes—all usually grown in a carefully tended plot in the back of the house. Alcott believed that manual labor and its resulting connection with nature was a way of building character.

In Concord, he immediately took a job as a woodcutter, work for which he was spectacularly unsuited. Not a strong man, his genius was in fanciful gardens and buildings, not in the necessary basics. He didn't cut much wood, but he reaped a harvest of good opinion in acting out what others saw as the role of philosopher and farmer, citizen and woodsman. Sixty-year-old William Ellery Channing, the Unitarian minister whose sons both became part of the Concord community, wrote to Elizabeth Peabody that "Alcott's combination of manual labor and intellectual energy made him the most interesting object in our Commonwealth."

Sometimes at dinner at the Alcott table, there was apple pudding with brown sugar for dessert. When the girls misbehaved, their father sent them to bed without dinner; when their misbehavior was more severe, he punished them by going without dinner himself.

At first, Bronson taught his girls a basic curriculum enhanced by large doses of Transcendental theory. "Vain is the hope of confirming a child in good habits," Alcott wrote, "while he is the subject of various influences over which the parent has no control."

Soon it was summertime. Louisa awoke to the sounds of a small New England village coming through the wide-open windows, a dog barking, the ping of the blacksmith's hammer, the clipping of horse's hooves as a carriage drove past, men's voices. We were fighting the Indians in Florida, and President Van Buren had sent troops to Maine to defend the frontier against the Aroostook Indians and the Canadians.

One morning, the bugles, drums, and fifes of the Townsend Light Infantry marched through Concord Center after a twenty-six-gun salute for the Fourth of July. Louisa watched the parade with her sisters, shouting as a log cabin drawn by oxen came rolling through Monument Square and along the Milldam, past Shattuck's store, which is now the Colonial Inn, and past banker Samuel Hoar's house and the store where J. W. Walcott sold coffee, tea, and sugar from the West Indies, past the dry-goods store and the bank and the Concord Gun Manufactory, where you could get everything from fowling pieces to six-barreled pistols. Banners and "Tippecanoe and Tyler Too" flags waved for the Whig Party candidacy of William Henry Harrison, called Old Tippecanoe for a battle he had won as a soldier fighting the Indians, and his vice president, John Tyler. Harrison and Tyler would win the election in November of 1840, but Harrison would be dead of pneumonia before he had served two months of his term, leaving Tyler to fill out his presidency.

4

LOUISA IN LOVE . . .
HENRY DAVID THOREAU

———◆———

One day the glamorous Margaret Fuller, dressed in chic Boston clothes, dropped by the Dovecote Cottage with Mr. Emerson. Miss Fuller was starting a new magazine, *The Dial*, and Alcott and Emerson were to be contributors. Fuller was staying at the Emersons', but when Emerson went around town on visits with Miss Fuller, Louisa noticed, his wife Lidian Emerson always stayed home. Fuller said she had come to see "Mr. Alcott's model children," but of course the moment she came was the moment that Louisa was galloping and stamping around the house and pawing the grass, doing one of her best horse imitations, allowing herself to be hitched up to little Anna's imaginary cart and then knocking them both down in a heap with their shoes off and their skirts flying.

"Here are the model children," Abba Alcott said to her guests with an edge to her voice that had become more and more pronounced. The adults were all talking about Miss Fuller's plans to go and live in nearby West Roxbury at the minister George Ripley's Brook Farm, the Utopian community. The idea of communities where everyone would share the labor and live in intellectual harmony was very much in the air of mid-century New England. Louisa could tell that her father didn't quite approve of Brook Farm.

As summer turned to autumn, Louisa found an adult who seemed to share her view of the world. Henry David Thoreau and his older brother John had started a small school in the town that was much like her father's old Temple School in Boston. Louisa and her sisters were enrolled. Louisa had often seen the Thoreau brothers, who seemed to spend a lot of time with a pretty adult named Ellen Sewall that summer. Now Ellen Sewall was gone, and the brothers had returned to expanding their teaching. Like the Alcotts, Thoreau was already dependent on Emerson, and Emerson urged Alcott to rely on Thoreau's teaching. Unlike Bronson, Thoreau used the natural world as his classroom, teaching his students about birdsong and flowers, about the cardinals and the finches and the way Indian pipe grew at the edge of the swamp. He would announce in the morning that he was taking his class to "heaven," and as Louisa and her classmates wandered behind him along the old Marlborough Road past the swamp or watched as Mr. Thoreau stripped some birch bark from a tree to make a basket for lichens they gathered, Louisa thought he had fulfilled his promise. Thoreau looked and moved as if he were still a child even though he was twenty-three years old and had already written a lot and graduated from Harvard. He had given a lecture on "Society" at the Concord Lyceum that Bronson Alcott had thought was good. But he was agile, short, and slight like a child. The only big things about Henry David Thoreau were his nose and his ideas.

Mr. Thoreau knew all the best places in the woods that Louisa had explored with what now seemed like blind eyes. He introduced his students to a family of chipmunks, coaxing one of the tiny creatures to take an acorn from his hand, and showed them how the chipmunks' underground house had a front and a back door hidden in the tall grass. He halted a daddy longlegs on its stilted way across a log, and showed them the ideal proportion of legs to body. Then he took them to the flat ponds in the swamp called Fairyland to see the water skaters. He pointed out a fox den at the side of an embankment and deer tracks in the mud near the turnpike and otter tracks along the riverbank. Following him, she found the best blackberries and blueberries, and even Indian arrowheads.

Sometimes he took them farther afield in an old hay wagon with a blanket spread over the hay for the children. He showed her a sparkling cobweb which he said was a handkerchief dropped by a fairy. He said that a birdsong was as wise as any philosophy. When her parents or her father and Emerson talked about Mr. Thoreau, they made him sound like an adult, obsessed with ideas and ways of making their idealism a daily practice. Louisa thought she knew him better.

Thoreau's boat the *Musketaquid,* which he and his brother had built with two masts for sailing and two sets of oars and a blue bottom to reflect the water and a green hull to mirror the trees, was another heavenly place. With Louisa in the front where she could see everything, Thoreau would push off into the river, and then they would just drift with the slow current, past Egg Rock, where the Sudbury River met the Assabet to make the Concord River, and under the willows and the place where the hemlocks swept down into the water. Mr. Thoreau explained that both the Sudbury and the Assabet rivers flowed into the Concord, which in turn flowed into the Merrimack farther north. He and his brother John were planning a trip in their boat from Concord, Massachusetts, north to Concord, New Hampshire, in August, he said. Louisa knew that the waters of the Merrimack had been tamed to give energy to the textile mills north of Concord, and that the young girls who worked in the mills came from all over the country. Her father had told the family about new laws protecting the young women under eighteen with minimum hour and wage regulations.

Louisa loved the way the still water reflected the maple and pin oaks along the bank as well as the passing clouds in the summer blue sky. When the sun went behind a cloud, she could see into the depths of the river, where fish beat slowly against the lazy current and green pondweed and fanwort waved against the sandy bottom. They passed the Old Manse, looking dark and forbidding above the meadow next to the river, which Thoreau explained was really a battlefield; and they slipped silently between the foundations of the Old North Bridge, which had been washed away. Pigeons were nesting in the crumbling abutments, and a family of wood ducks swirled around the boat. A line of turtles napped on a fallen log that jutted out into the silky water. Thoreau made the first shots of the Revolutionary War come to life as he explained where the farmer soldiers had stood to defend their freedom. He showed her how the white pond lilies clustered near the shore near the duckweed and water shield. He leaned out of the boat and caught a small trout in his hands, let the sun shimmer against its scales, and then let it go. In Mr. Thoreau's company, the world seemed alive with animals; he pointed out kingfishers and herons she would never have seen and showed her how a pile of logs at the side of the river was really a huge beaver dam. What had at first seemed bunches of twigs were the nests of the great blue herons.

The boat glided along the glassy surface, pushed along by Mr. Thoreau's flowing pull against the narrow paddle, which made a slight, musical sucking sound as he slid it in and out of the still water. He would fall into a special silence, and Louisa knew she should keep her eyes open for a heron, a huge prehistoric-looking bird, standing on one impossibly long stick of a leg, or a great horned owl lurking in the weeds near the water. In the romantic, enclosed world of the little boat, Louisa gathered impressions so vivid and passionate that they would appear and reappear in her work. Boat trips on the river are the narrative thread of Thoreau's first work—*A Week on the Concord and Merrimack Rivers*—and of the novel Louisa May Alcott considered her best work, the now-forgotten *Moods*.

5

SIC VITA

———◆———

Henry David Thoreau's first love poem was not written to the admiring young Louisa May Alcott. It was wrapped around a bunch of freshly picked violets, tied neatly with a blade of green grass, and tossed through the paned ground-floor window at the Parkman House into the bedroom occupied by Lucy Jackson Brown. It was one of those glorious early spring mornings in Concord. The last of the snow melt had filled the rivers to their grassy banks and left surprising green everywhere. The snowdrops bordered the dirt road, and the woods were filled with myrtle and the first early ferns and wild cabbages. The jellied pads of frog's eggs floated downstream, and earlier that day he had seen the first trout fingerlings and tadpoles near the riverbank.

The dew was still on the grass as the smitten Harvard senior gathered the flowers. He could hear a jay screaming in the elm tree above him—*phe-phay, phe-phay*—and the loud, shrill phoebe and the chickadees pecking at the seeds in the gravel at the edge of the dirt road. As he approached the house, he could smell his mother's bread baking in the big kitchen where his sisters Sophia and Helen were preparing the midday meal—one of his mother's vegetable soups with bread and butter made from the Hosmers' cows. He could hear the thump of the pencil-making machines in the sheds beyond. Thoreau pencils were good pencils, as good as Mason or Dixon pencils, he knew, but they still hadn't succeeded in equaling the fine, firm leads of the Faber pencils imported from Germany.

Thoreau's grandfather had come from St. Heliers in Jersey, off the coast of Normandy, to Boston and started the pencil-making business, but although his father worked hard, the business had never quite yielded enough to support the four Thoreau children. Henry had grown up in the sheds, playing with discarded plumbago—the dark powder used to make leads—and sawdust, and at his parents' boardinghouse table playing with all kinds of people who came to Concord for its exalted Revolutionary War history, for the great Ralph Waldo Emerson, and for its breathtaking natural beauty.

Sic Vita was the poem's title, and its cadence doesn't do a lot of credit to the Harvard education he had just completed, his brilliance as a Greek scholar, or the knowledge of Goethe, Virgil, and Aristotle which was common among his classmates. As always with Thoreau, the poem is more about the natural world than the world of the human heart. It's about the violets that went with it and less about the feelings that may have gone with it.

> *I am a parcel of vain strivings tied*
> *By a chance bond together,*
> *Dangling this way and that, their links*
> *Were made so loose and wide,*
> *Methinks,*
> *For milder weather.*

There had been many boarders at the Thoreaus' house over the years, but Lucy Brown's aloneness in the world with her son and daughter had captivated him. She was a literary woman of a certain age on a protracted visit to her sister Lidian, who had married the local sage, Ralph Waldo Emerson, and moved into a big square white house with him on the other side of town. The Emerson House—formerly called the Coolidge Castle after the man who built it—was big but not quite big enough for the Great Emerson, his second wife, and her sharp-tongued older sister with her two young children. Lucy Brown was twenty years older than the young Thoreau, a woman of the world who had married a Boston merchant. After being caught in some shady dealings, which were never spoken of, he fled to Europe, leaving his family behind. She came to Concord at the Emersons' invitation, and moved for a while into the rambling white Thoreau House at the corner on Parkman Street.

At the boardinghouse, Lucy Brown was enchanted with the Thoreau family and especially with Henry and John's younger sister Sophia, who helped her parents run the place. One night she took Sophia to hear her brilliant brother-in-law give a speech on manners at the Concord Lyceum. During the lecture, Sophia leaned forward and whispered to her hostess that her brother had recently written an essay including some of the same ideas.

Both men opposed the inherited authority of the Puritans; both searched for a looser, more human and natural idea of God. Lucy brought a few of Thoreau's essays to her brother-in-law, and a meeting was arranged. In fact, Emerson, working behind the scenes, had already helped Thoreau win badly needed scholarship money at Harvard. The financial support that was the hallmark of Emerson's connections to almost everyone he knew had already begun before he even met the young Thoreau. Thoreau had read and admired Emerson's essay *Nature*.

So on a Sunday morning in 1837, Thoreau set out with Lucy Brown for the walk across Concord from the Thoreaus' boardinghouse to the Emerson House. As they passed the schoolhouse, Thoreau paused to hear the first bobolink's flashing, tinkling notes and to point out the ready-to-burst apple blossoms. They must have made an odd pair as they sauntered down the Sudbury Road and walked down Main Street and over the Milldam.

They passed the great Concord Elm and the Monument to the Revolutionary War Dead at the oblong town green, and the shops where the Thoreaus bought their groceries and had their horses shod. The blacksmith was already hammering, and a burst of heat and the smell of scorched metal billowed out into the fragrant, apple-blossom air of a New England spring. They went right by the house that Lucy Brown would rent when she came back to Concord with her children in 1841, and took a right at the First Parish Church toward the Cambridge Turnpike, where the Emerson House sits on a low piece of ground bordered by marshes and shaded by trees. In the soft edge of the road, Thoreau could see partridge tracks and the scratching tracks of some sparrows next to the oblong hoof marks of a family of deer.

Lucy Brown was a slender woman, older and more glamorous than her plainer sister Lydia, who had become Lidian Emerson at the advanced age of thirty-six after meeting the great man during a lecture series in her hometown of Plymouth on Cape Cod. Lucy Brown was an outsider now too, a woman whose best efforts at leading a conventional life had gone dreadfully astray, a single mother in a time before single mothers.

Thoreau had always been an outsider. He seemed to have been born to an unconventional life. From the beginning, it was clear that the boy christened David Henry was an exceptional boy. As part of their spirit of reinvention, their sense of rediscovering the universe afresh, many of the Concord writers changed their names. Lydia Jackson became Lidian. David Henry Thoreau became Henry David. Bronson Alcott changed Alcox to Alcott and Hawthorne added the *w* to his family name of Hathorne.

While Thoreau's parents worried about the price of room and board and what to serve at the communal table, Henry was reading Plato and wondering about the relationship between man and nature. Always uncomfortable with people, he seemed more at home with ideas and even more at home in his beloved woods or out on the river. He never seemed to care how he looked. His wild hair, shabby clothes, and scuffed boots were added to his disdain for personal hygiene. He walked fast, often getting ahead of companions, and looked steadfastly at the ground. Hawthorne said he was "as ugly as sin"; Oliver Wendell Holmes complained about his bad table manners—Thoreau liked to eat with his fingers. For the smitten Louisa May Alcott, Thoreau's obnoxious surface was part of his charm, as she later wrote: "Beneath the defects the Master's eye saw the grand lines that were to serve as the model for the perfect man."

6

TWO LOVES

———◆———

Henry David Thoreau opened the white wooden gate for his companion, and they walked across the lawn toward the Greek Revival portico over the front door and entered the sanctum sanctorum of the Emerson household. Ushered into Emerson's study, Thoreau sat on the edge of a chair like a trapped animal while Lucy went upstairs to visit with her sister and baby Waldo, the Emersons' first child, born the year before.

The visit went well. Thoreau's cascades of conversation, jeweled with his own ideas about the nature of man and the place of man in nature, soon charmed Emerson. Even as they began forming a community, they shared contempt for manufactured communities like George Ripley's Brook Farm, which was being established in Roxbury. "I'd rather keep a bachelor's board in hell than go to board in heaven," Thoreau quipped. Once he relaxed, Thoreau said whatever came into his head, and he had an ability to surprise with wit and honesty that Emerson, fourteen years older, immediately prized. He laughed at Thoreau's theory that man had mistaken the godly order of things and that man should labor on the seventh day and rest for the other six. Both men were fascinated by Eastern writings and religions, beginning with the Upanishads. Thoreau had translated from the French *The Transmigration of the Seven Brahmins,* and explained to Emerson the Laws of Manu with their invocations to silence and closeness with nature.

Both were Harvard men, both had strolled across the Yard and felt the thrill of a community of scholars. Emerson was not exactly a loyal alumnus. Already in the spring of 1837, he had left the ministry after a severe disagreement with his parishioners. By the next year, with a speech to the graduating Divinity School seniors in July of 1838, Emerson would shock the Harvard powers that be so profoundly with his attack on the formal church and his praise of human intuition that he would be banned from his own alma mater for the next twenty-five years. He wasn't invited back until 1865, after the Civil War had changed everything, when he was asked to take part in a memorial service for the soldiers.

For Thoreau, at last in the company of someone who was equally learned and equally unconventional, as well as being established and respected, this afternoon with Emerson was the beginning of the intellectual life he had dreamed of. Emerson urged him to start keeping a journal, and he began the almost daily entries that would result in the most complete record of the Concord community in existence. He began to imitate Emerson's accent and Emerson's hand gestures, and even Emerson's clothing. He fell in love with Emerson and his family that afternoon, with the big house and its capacious grounds, gardens, and orchards, and with the first Emerson child. He was already half in love with Lucy, and now he added her family to his heart, including her sister Lidian and the great man himself.

During the twenty-five years of their friendship, years of real intimacy as Thoreau took over Emerson's household and fell in love with his wife, years in which Emerson supported Thoreau financially, years of intellectual companionship and growth, Thoreau was always the disciple in a way that may have overshadowed him as much as it helped him. Not until long, long after the publication of his greatest work, *Walden,* about a house built with a loan from Emerson on land owned by Emerson, did Thoreau escape the gossipy assumption that he was more Emerson's man than his own. Their contemporary James Russell Lowell wrote a mean poem about Thoreau that reflected the opinion of many of their peers and townspeople:

> *He follows as close as a stick to a rocket,*
> *His fingers exploring the prophet's each pocket.*
> *Fie, for shame, brother bard; with good fruit of your own,*
> *Can't you let Neighbor Emerson's orchards alone?*

Thoreau's second love poem was written in June two years later to one of his students, Edmund Sewall. *Sympathy,* which was later published in *The Dial,* was both more graphic and less lighthearted than *Sic Vita.* Thoreau loved his students. At first, he had been a reluctant schoolteacher, who began his career at the Concord Public Free School the fall he graduated from Harvard. What else could he do? On the first day, he announced to his class that he didn't believe in flogging. He said he would talk morals as a punishment instead. Two weeks into the school year, the deacon of the school complained that Thoreau's class was unruly. What he meant by that was that the students were excited about the material they were learning; they didn't have the half-dead look of the well-behaved students of the time, learning facts and figures by rote and discouraged from any kind of thoughtful enthusiasm. He ordered the gentle Thoreau to flog his students. Apparently, this sent Thoreau into a tantrum of angry obedience; he flogged six students with the ruler and summarily resigned his post as a teacher.

Undeterred, he then applied for other teaching jobs in Massachusetts, New Hampshire, and Maine, finally starting a school of his own in the Parkman House, where his parents also took in boarders. In 1838, he was able to take over the failing Concord Academy across the street and make enough of a success with his strange alternative methods—many of them copied from Bronson Alcott's Temple School—that he could even hire his brother John. The two brothers had always been close—Henry called John his "good genius"—and the school was a perfect forum for their complementary personalities, John the friendly, open older one, and Henry the expert and intellectual who sometimes seemed cold but could always come up with a new fact, or way of looking at things, or just the piece of information that turned a muddy bog into a story about the animals that had been there to drink. Born in July, Henry was as irritable as he was passionate. *"Spes sibi quisque,"* he would tell the students quoting his beloved Virgil—"Each one his own hope." His brother John was taller, handsomer, and more conventional.

John, using the downstairs room at the academy, taught English and mathematics. Henry upstairs taught Latin, Greek, physics, and natural history. The school was devoted to learning by doing, a solid progressive idea, and at least once a week the two masters led their students, whooping for joy and hollering at the freedom of being out of the classroom, for a walk in the woods or an outing on the river or the ponds in the brothers' boat. The students clamored to walk with Henry, who knew so much about Concord that his knowledge seemed magical—some of his students thought he must have made the place because he knew so much about it. He knew the calls of all the birds, the habits of the trees and flowers. He could reach out and catch a frog and pet it as if it were a house cat.

Once he took a group of students sailing down the Sudbury River past its juncture with the Assabet and on down the Concord River past the wide marshes called the Great Meadows and landed on the river shore apparently at random. He led the students through a discussion of the Wampanoag Indians on the spot, speculating that this would be a good camping place since it provided fish, woods, a fresh spring for water, and shelter from the winds. He talked about the Wampanoag sachem Alexander, one of Massasoit's two sons, and the way he had died after a visit to the Plymouth Bay Colony, which made his brother Philip think he had been poisoned. A decade later, Philip's anger spilled into open war between the Indians and the settlers. With a spade, Thoreau began to dig, and just when everyone had lost interest, his spade struck a fire-marked stone which was part of a circle that marked an ancient fireplace.

Thoreau took a group of boys to watch the typesetters work at the local newspaper; he had a plot of land for each student to plant a personal garden, and took them out to Fairhaven Bay with a leveler and a surveyor's tool to have them practice the mathematics of surveying. One afternoon, the students heard some chirping sounds near Goose Pond. "It has been disputed whether the noise was caused by frogs," wrote Edmund Sewall, one of the academy's students and Thoreau's favorite. "Mr. Thoreau however caught three very small frogs, two of them in the act of chirping. While bringing them home one of them chirped in his hat. He carried them to Mr. Emerson in a tumbler of water. They chirped there also."

Young Sewall, a student from Scituate, Massachusetts, the son of the town's pastor, the Reverend Edmund Quincy Sewall, was the grandson of Mrs. Joseph Ward, who lived in the Thoreau boardinghouse. Sewall, age eleven, had come for a visit to his grandmother and been enchanted by the Thoreaus, who took him sailing and berry-picking. Edmund wanted nothing more than to return to the Thoreaus and Concord Academy. The feeling was mutual. In the poem that has been interpreted variously by generations of Thoreau scholars as platonic, sexual, and expressing desire for a woman disguised as a man, Henry wrote, "Lately, alas, I knew a gentle boy," and continued in a vague and mannered tribute to a young man. Edmund got his wish and became a boarding student at Concord Academy for the following year.

The poem, ostensibly written to a boy, certainly led to a girl. When Edmund's sister, seventeen-year-old Ellen, came to visit a few weeks later on July 20, to stay with her grandmother and her Aunt Prudence, the Thoreau brothers forgot all about Edmund Sewall, and almost everything else. Ellen Sewall's visit was the beginning of a slow explosion of passion and agony between the two brothers that never really healed and that reverberated in the hearts of everyone close to them.

7

ELLEN SEWALL

———◆———

Both brothers seem to have fallen immediately in love with the slender, beautiful Ellen, and she with both of them. "There is no remedy for love than to love more," Henry wrote ecstatically in his journals. Soon enough, he was rowing between the Concord River's grassy banks while Ellen, her hair braided and her pretty face shaded by a wide hat, reclined on cushions in the stern. Time stopped in the steamy August afternoons, butterflies flitted in the purple loosestrife. Enchanted, Henry let the boat drift and taught her to listen for the cool water twitter of the goldfinch and the blackbird's harsh *char-char-char*.

Under the green of the weeping willows, across the Fairhaven Lake, talking softly or just in companionable silence, their hearts beat to the rhythm of Henry's oars. Ellen leaned over to dangle a hand in the water. Sometimes, Henry stopped to show her something on the riverbank or in the clear, cool summer water. Near Egg Rock, they surprised a great blue heron who rose from the marshes and soared off down the river. "Surely joy is the condition of life," he wrote in his journal. "Think of the young fry that leap into ponds—the myriads of insects ushered into being of a summer's evening—the incessant note of the hyla with which the woods ring in the spring, the nonchalance of the butterfly carrying accident and change painted in a thousand hues upon his wings—or the brook minnow stemming stoutly the current, the luster of whose scales worn bright by the attrition is reflected upon the bank."

Each brother courted the same woman in his own way. John paid calls on Ellen and exchanged polite conversation. Henry walked Ellen up to the Fairhaven Cliffs, where he played the flute for her and escorted her through the woods to Walden Pond. Ellen had other suitors in Concord—a Harvard student named John Keynes even managed to walk her home after a party one night—but the Thoreau brothers were her constant companions. They boated on the river together, found Indian arrowheads half-buried in the woods, went to parties and picnics, and were amazed at a giraffe that came to Concord with a traveling show.

Ellen went back to Scituate at the end of August, leaving each brother with his own vivid hopes and dreams. But John was the practical brother. When the two brothers discovered that Ellen had left her collection of arrowheads behind, Henry was hurt; John packed them up and sent them off to Scituate with a love letter.

Starting on the last day of August, the two men set out from Concord on a long-planned river trip to paddle north up to the sources of the Concord and the Merrimack. They were able to paddle upstream with a few portages—their boat had been ingeniously built with small wheels to make overland hauls easier. It was a wonderful trip, but their mutual feelings for the same woman seemed to lie unspoken between them like an unwelcome third party. The morning they got home, almost before the boat was tied up, John packed his bags and left to visit Ellen in Scituate.

The elder Sewalls were away, and John and Ellen spent most of two days together. John came home feeling lighthearted, encouraged by the obvious affection that Ellen had shown for him during his visit. In spite of his own longings, Henry officially deferred to his older brothers' courtship. During the late summer and fall of 1840, Thoreau allowed the little girl Louisa May Alcott's adoration to soften the blows of an adult love triangle that would also haunt Louisa's mature work.

At Christmastime, the two brothers traveled to Scituate for a visit, and once again the three of them found themselves with hundreds of things to talk and laugh about. John was gaining the upper hand. When they got home, both brothers sent Ellen gifts—John a collection of beautiful opals and a bold admonition to Ellen's little brother Georgie to give her a New Year's kiss for him, and Henry a volume of poetry by his friend Jones Very and some of his own precious poems. Ellen wrote back thanking John and only John. In June, Ellen came to Concord and went on long boat trips with Henry and walks with John, encouraging him so completely that a few weeks later he traveled up to Scituate for the purpose of proposing.

On a walk along the lovely beach looking out at the islands in Massachusetts Bay, John asked Ellen Sewall to be his wife. It was a summer day, the ocean whispered against the sand, and she could see the ledges of Cohasset off in the distance and a few clouds high in a blue sky. Carried away by the moment, she accepted his offer and agreed to become Mrs. John Thoreau.

Later that afternoon when the couple returned to the Sewall house and an elated John Thoreau formally asked the Reverend Sewall for his daughter's hand in marriage, things went wrong. He was summarily rejected. The Reverend Sewall didn't approve of his lovely young daughter linking her life with that of a young halfhearted schoolteacher from Concord with few important prospects. There was much angry discussion behind closed doors.

Painfully, without much explanation, Ellen then rescinded her acceptance in a few words. She couldn't go against her parents, she said. What was even more painful was that she appeared to be more relieved than heartbroken. John returned home to Concord depressed and confused.

After the embarrassment of John's proposal and Ellen's acceptance, Ellen's parents quickly decided she needed a change of scene. There would be no more visits to Concord, no more innocent threesomes on the river or at the Thoreau family table. Instead, they sent her to Watertown, New York, to stay with a cousin. She was out of sight but hardly out of mind for the Thoreau brothers. The heartbroken John began to accept his loss, but Henry's feelings were furiously mixed. He was loyal to his brother and outraged on John's behalf. On the other hand, he was still in love with Ellen. In one October letter to her Aunt Prudence, she asked specifically about Henry: "What great work is Henry engaged in now?"

With a boldness that he would never find again in human company, Henry wrote Ellen proposing marriage. She rejected him by return mail showing a lightheartedness that felt like cruelty. At least, she wrote, he had had the good sense to put his proposal in a letter and not to confront her during a walk on a beach.

8

MONEY

———◆———

Ralph Waldo Emerson had grown up in Boston; he was born on May 25, 1803, in a house at the corner of Sumner and Chauncy streets, a little more than a year before the birth of Nathaniel Hawthorne. The United States was in its infancy, hanging on by pure stubbornness after a mere twenty-five years of existence, with no real capital, rickety finances, and a sharp understanding that its only claims to fame were equality for white men and vast expanses of land—neither of which seemed like an unmixed asset. Boston itself was a small town with a few more than 25,000 residents, a dwarf next to the already great cities of London and Paris.

Emerson's father was the Reverend William Emerson, the minister of First Church, Boston—his salary was twenty-five dollars a week, thirty cords of wood a year, and the use of a house. The family was already too poor for frills, and with the death of William Emerson when Ralph Waldo was eight, his mother was left with limited resources for raising a family of six children. A deeply religious woman, she took in boarders and desperately tried to find ways to get an education for her adored sons, enlisting friends to tutor them for Harvard. Emerson's Aunt Mary Moody Emerson, an educated woman and a skillful writer, was welcomed as a surrogate parent for the boys. An eccentric single woman who, by choice, never married, Mary Moody Emerson was as honest as she was smart. Her obituary noted that "she was thought to have the power of saying more disagreeable things in half an hour than any person living." Ralph was the third of six sons, the one with the sense of humor, but it was hard to laugh at the Emersons' situation.

Three of Emerson's siblings died during childhood and two before age thirty. Another, Bulkeley, was mentally handicapped. The family was so poor that neighbors and friends often gave them loans to survive. Emerson remembered one long winter when he and his older brother, Edward, shared an overcoat. His mother had some help from Mary Moody Emerson, who took a liking to Ralph Waldo and started him reading. Because of her influence, Emerson was able to go to the Boston Latin School and finally enter Harvard College.

At college, he was an average student; he was chosen class poet but only after six other students had declined the offer. He formed a club for public speaking and was good at oratory, with a deep, well-modulated baritone voice. When he graduated after making some money teaching and writing, he decided to become a minister. In 1826, the Middlesex Association of Ministers licensed him to preach, and he gave his first sermon in Waltham, Massachusetts. While preaching in Concord, New Hampshire, he met pretty, wealthy Ellen Tucker and fell deeply in love.

In marrying Ellen Tucker, Emerson had seemed to resolve his financial and emotional problems. All seemed to have turned out well in spite of the wounds of his childhood. He was home safe. They laid their happy plans. Ellen loved writing, and she would be a poet while Emerson took over a pulpit of the Second Unitarian Church in Boston's North End and preached rousing sermons. She was eighteen when they were married. But from the beginning, Ellen had a terrible cough, which progressed to advanced tuberculosis. In spite of everything that could be done for tuberculosis in those days—the long open-air carriage rides and the huge doses of country air—the disease killed her when she was just twenty. Ellen's death undid Emerson. At twenty-eight, he had a vocational and personal meltdown, visiting Ellen's grave every day—once even opening her coffin to see for himself that she was dead and to be closer to her—and finally resigning his ministry. How could he believe that Ellen was dead when he seemed to be speaking and writing to her in the same way he always had? How could he have faith in a God who would allow the shattering of their young lives?

In June of 1832, he rebelled against what he saw as his parishioners' dependence on communion at the expense of acting out Christ's teachings in their everyday lives. He saw them going to church as a fulfillment of their obligations and forgetting about the quality of their behavior the rest of the week. Already he was beginning to turn away from the rigid structure of the Christian Trinity and find spiritual solace in other people, in the natural world, and in his own breaking heart. He came to the point where he no longer believed that Christ had intended a weekly communion in memory of the last supper. "I think Jesus did not mean to institute a perpetual celebration," he wrote in a letter to his congregation explaining that he could no longer celebrate the Eucharist. He offered to continue preaching at services that did not have communion, the center of the church service. The church rejected his proposal. So he preached a last sermon, left the church, and left the country to travel for a while. He visited France, Italy, and England, where he met Thomas Carlyle, Coleridge, and Wordsworth.

He came home in 1833 a wiser and bolder thinker and a man with more faith in individual intuition than in the rules and regulations of distinguished institutions. "In all of my lectures," he wrote in his journal in 1840, "I have preached one doctrine, namely, the infinitude of the private man." In the late 1830s, the new apostate published his essay *Nature* and gave two lectures at Harvard that were to become famous. One, "The American Scholar," was called by Oliver Wendell Holmes "the declaration of independence of American intellectual life."

"Meek young men grow up in libraries," he told his shocked audience at Harvard's Phi Beta Kappa Society on August 31, 1837, "believing it their duty to accept the views which Cicero, which Locke, which Bacon, have given, forgetful that Cicero, Locke and Bacon were only young men in libraries when they wrote these books."

The following year, Emerson was invited to speak at the Harvard Divinity School, where his attack on "historical Christianity" so offended the Divinity School faculty that he was purposefully excluded from Harvard for decades.

9

EMERSON PAYS FOR
EVERYTHING

———◆———

Emerson had loved Ellen profoundly, but he did not love poverty, however genteel. On her deathbed, Ellen Tucker had said that she could do him "more good by going than by staying." One interpretation of this had to do with her wealth. Emerson clearly felt that although Ellen had died at the age of twenty—not yet officially an adult—she had meant the money to go to him for his many good works. Although Emerson had no intention of acting against Ellen Tucker's grieving mother and sister, her sister's husband's claims were a completely different story. At a time when family matters rarely ended up before a judge, Emerson angrily took the Tuckers to court. He won. The Massachusetts Supreme Court in Chancery agreed that Emerson should receive Ellen's portion of the Tucker wealth.

Without this obscure lawsuit in 1836, it's hard to know what would have happened in Concord, Massachusetts, if anything. It was Ellen Tucker's share of the Tuckers' fortune that bought the Emerson House on the Cambridge Turnpike and was sustaining the Alcotts as well as the Hawthornes and Henry David Thoreau. Emerson not only paid the rent; Louisa noticed that after a visit from Mr. Emerson there was often a small pile of bills under a candlestick on the dining room table, or left on top of a pile of books he had brought from his library.

As far as Louisa could tell, Emerson and his second wife, the practical Lidian, got along well. She called him Mr. Emerson, or in a lighter mood "O King!" He often called her his Lidian Queen, or Queenie for short. Lidian Emerson didn't allow smoking in the house, and Louisa was delighted to see Emerson hiding a half-smoked cigar under the railing of the fence before going indoors. Emerson's courtship of his second wife, originally named Lydia Jackson, a Cape Cod woman a year older than himself, had been one of the first steps he took to build the literary community he instinctively knew might replace the family he had lost.

"I obey my highest impulses in declaring to you the feeling of deep and tender respect with which you have inspired me," he began the letter with which he made his marriage proposal. The letter, which does not mention the word marriage, explains that he did not make the proposal in person because he did not have time. Did Lydia Jackson know how much this would set the tone for their marriage? Apparently not. During 1834, Emerson had made three visits to the small town of Plymouth, twice as a guest preacher and once to give a lecture to the townspeople.

His audience each time included a slender woman with wide gray eyes who lived in a large house with gardens and who, at age thirty-two, had come to seem happy with her spinster state. She had lost both her parents within three months in 1818. Her sister Lucy had made an unfortunate marriage and was trying to raise two children on her own and in straitened circumstances hampered by scandal, and her geologist brother Charles had recently married.

Emerson, however, got her attention. Tall, handsome, brilliant, and single, with a deep, dreamy baritone voice and a kind of certainty about spiritual matters that could make what had been a happy life seem absurdly narrow, Emerson soon infiltrated Lydia Jackson's dreams. She even had a shocking daydream in which she saw herself going downstairs to be married to him. She couldn't stop thinking about him. After another lecture in Plymouth in January 1835, Lydia stayed around for the party afterward and actually had a conversation with the man of her dreams. What passed between them? Whatever it was, it was momentous. The next afternoon, a letter was delivered to Lydia addressed in an unfamiliar handwriting. It was Emerson's marriage proposal.

In fact, as she read his letter, he had already left Plymouth. From out of town he urged her to answer his proposal with her own letter to him. Emerson wasn't taking any chances. He had lost enough. He had been poor. He had been robbed, and he had learned to fight back. Lydia said yes, and Emerson traveled back to Plymouth to talk with her. Although she shrank, she told him, from the "load of care and labor" that marrying him would entail, she would happily bear the load if he loved and needed her. Did he ever; did he ever! Now, in the sandy soil of Lydia Jackson's feelings and on the marshy grass around the white house, he would build his foundation. Gently, Emerson proposed that she change her name to Lidian. She agreed to all of it.

In the thrilling presence of the slender, six-foot-tall Emerson, she couldn't know how homesick she would be for coastal Plymouth in the landlocked, rural lanes of Concord. She couldn't see that Emerson would be away giving lectures a great deal of the time—sometimes in Boston and sometimes in London—and that she would be left to run a household filled with unruly children and guests; bedeviled by maids who were more trouble than they were worth; belittled by Emerson's aging mother, Ruth Haskins Emerson, who lived with them; paying off creditors to keep the whole leaky ship afloat; dealing when the "great man" was in residence with Emerson's "friendships" with other women; and finally being consoled by none other than Henry David Thoreau, the one human being on earth who seemed to see her clearly.

Of the five writers who happened to live in Concord and at one time or another at the crossroads of the Lexington Road and the Cambridge Turnpike, Emerson was the most conservative, his writing the most austere, but his money—made from incessant lecturing and inherited through the dead Ellen Tucker—supported them all. He paid the Alcotts' rent and was almost always available for borrowing for a worthy cause like the purchase of a farmhouse and land for Alcott's community, Fruitlands—Emerson drew up the deed—or a ticket to England for Alcott when things were going badly in New England. He also supported Hawthorne, although somewhat less directly. It was Emerson who enabled the Hawthornes finally to get married after three years of secret engagement by persuading his cousin Samuel Ripley to rent the Old Manse, having Thoreau dig and plant the garden for them, and making gifts and loans during the three years that the Hawthornes lived in Concord and were dogged by severe poverty. Emerson helped bring the Hawthornes back to Concord years later after they had lived abroad.

He helped support the perpetually, proudly impoverished Thoreau, finding him work, getting him published, providing him with limitless loans, and finally lending him the woodlot on Walden Pond. When he was staying with his own family, Thoreau paid regular rent. At the Emersons', his help around the house was enough of a contribution. Another beneficiary, Margaret Fuller, was editor of *The Dial* because of Emerson, and she often lived at the Emersons' house and was always welcome there. He loaned books, he opened his doors if not quite completely his heart, and he handed out money.

Emerson wrote some wonderful lines, and some true biographical portraits, but it is as the sugar daddy of American literature that he really takes his place in the pantheon of Concord writers. He married a practical woman and established their home in a way that welcomed all comers. Then he began reaching out, first to his wife's sister, then to Thoreau, then the Alcotts, and later to Jones Very, the young poet who sometimes thought he was Jesus Christ, and to the Hawthornes. It was Emerson who kept ties with Longfellow and Oliver Wendell Holmes in Boston, but also Emerson who invited the Peabody sisters to be part of the Concord circle and who made sure that Thoreau met Walt Whitman and Edgar Allan Poe when he was in New York City.

Emerson asked Franklin Sanborn to come and start a school in Concord in 1855, and kept up a friendship with Thomas Wentworth Higginson in Amherst. When Higginson's young friend Emily Dickinson sent Higginson her first poems, he didn't know what to think. He forwarded them to Emerson, who wrote back that he didn't think much of them. Emerson kept up connections with writers such as Carlyle and Coleridge in England, and he had a hand in bringing John Brown to Concord, where he had assembled a group of men and women who were sure to support him.

10

TWO DEATHS

———◆———

As it turned out, neither of the two Thoreau brothers was to marry Ellen Sewall or anyone else, ever. A few years after her rejection of John and then Henry, in 1844, Ellen Sewall married a minister, the Reverend Joseph Osgood from her hometown of Scituate; she raised a family and presumably never looked back on the golden summers in Concord she had shared with the impoverished, eccentric, entertaining brothers Thoreau.

The transition was not so easy for the Thoreaus. Henry sank into a depression so severe that even his new friend Emerson noticed. Perhaps Thoreau needed a rest from his own family, Emerson suggested. Emerson offered Thoreau a room in the Emerson House, an alcove at the top of the stairs where Thoreau could write in peace. On April 18 of 1841, Thoreau moved into the Emerson House and into a second painful love triangle, one which, when it disintegrated—and don't they always disintegrate?—would catapult him into a new level of writing.

At first, things went well at the Emersons', beginning the two years that would be one of the high points of Emerson's friendship with Thoreau. Emerson was famously clumsy, and Thoreau quickly set to work doing the chores Emerson couldn't handle. He planted the Emersons' garden, pruned the orchard, and cleaned out the chimneys. The spring days were filled with the satisfying sound of Thoreau working with a hammer and saw, or with the spade and hoe.

When Lidian Emerson, who was passionately grateful for Thoreau's practical and fascinating presence, needed a place to store her gloves for church, Thoreau built a special compartment under the seat of a dining room chair. He couldn't do enough for her. When Emerson was off on the lecture tours—and he was gone with more and more frequency—he felt assured that his wife and children were in good hands. Thoreau listened to Lidian in a way that was thrilling and strange for her, and she lit up when he walked into a room.

Thoreau was also a special hit with the Emerson children, the baby Edith and the beloved five-year-old Waldo. He made Waldo popguns and whistles and boats, took him for walks in the woods, showing him tiny animals he had never noticed before, and treated him with a respectful firmness. For Thoreau, the arrangement was perfect, especially when Emerson was away. He had full access to Emerson's rich library, the fun of playing with children and doing handiwork, and the admiration of a woman whose friendship made her beautiful when he was in the same room.

No one knew that John Thoreau would be dead within the year, killed by a case of lockjaw, or tetanus, contracted when he cut himself while shaving. On New Year's Day of 1842, John was stropping his razor when it slipped and nicked the ring finger of his left hand. He put on a bandage and forgot about it, but when he removed the bandage a week later, the skin looked strange enough for him to call on Dr. Josiah Bartlett, who redressed the wound but thought nothing of it. On the way home, John was seized with severe aches and pains, and before that night lockjaw had set in. Henry moved out of the Emersons' and back into his family house to take care of his brother night and day, holding him through his delirious times and keeping him company when the pain seemed to lift. John died early in the morning of January 11 in Henry's arms.

It was an awful month at the Emerson House. Thoreau had gone home to nurse John, and now the Emersons heard that he had the symptoms of lockjaw too. Henry had a "sympathetic" attack; it passed. It looked as if he too was going to die, if only of heartbreak. He was jolted into health on January 24 when Waldo Emerson came down with scarlet fever. The little boy was dead within three days. Thoreau had come to love Waldo also, and the whole big white house seemed to shake and tremble with grief.

Emerson wrote for all of them in a letter to Margaret Fuller about

Waldo's death. "My little boy must die also. All his wonderful beauty, could not save him. He gave up his innocent breath last night and my world this morning is poor enough. He had scarlatina on Monday night. Shall I ever dare to love anything again. Farewell and farewell, O my Boy!"

John Thoreau, in a playful moment in the fall, had taken Waldo to sit for a daguerreotypist—now the tiny image was all that was left of either of them.

These two awful deaths sent Lidian Emerson into years of depression and bitterness, alleviated only by her interest in gardening. Thoreau was one of the few people she could bear to have around. Emerson was devastated, and this also told on his friendship with the young man who was sharing his house. For the first time, but not for the last, Thoreau and Emerson seemed to lose their connection. "My friend is cold and reserved because his love for me is waxing and not waning," wrote the understanding Thoreau on March 20. "These are the early processes; the particles are just beginning to shoot into crystals."

11

THE CURSE OF SALEM

———◆———

Nathaniel Hawthorne had grown up in Salem, Massachusetts, in a house he called "Castle Dismal" on Herbert Street overlooking the village cemetery. His father was a sailor who died of yellow fever in Surinam when he was eight, and Hawthorne, who was largely raised by his sisters Elizabeth and Mary, went to Bowdoin College before returning to Salem to become, he hoped, a writer.

If Concord with its grassy rivers and great elms was heaven, Salem was a kind of hell. The memory of the witch trials in which 19 people were hanged on Gallows Hill, 1 tortured to death, and 150 imprisoned was fresh everywhere when Hawthorne was growing up. His grandfather John Hathorne had been one of the judges, a judge who, legend has it, was personally cursed as one of the so-called witches mounted the scaffold to be killed by his neighbors. "God will give him blood to drink," Hawthorne's Matthew Maule spits out as he is hanged as a witch in *The House of the Seven Gables*.

The shadow of what happened in Salem haunted American literature for generations, providing parables for writers such as Oliver Wendell Holmes, John Greenleaf Whittier, and Henry Wadsworth Longfellow as well as for playwright Arthur Miller, who adapted the story in his play *The Crucible* to dramatize his views on the Army-McCarthy Hearings of the Senate Permanent Committee on Investigations in the 1950s. There was no getting over what had happened in the town where Hawthorne grew up, walking over the hill named for his ancestors and being surrounded with reminders of that dreadful winter.

Even now, more than 150 years after Hawthorne lived in Salem, the town is a strange place, a mixture of honky-tonk, like the witchcraft museum that features dioramas of people being hanged or failing to say the Lord's Prayer or being brought before the full court of judges, and solemn horror like the quiet stones placed in memory of those murdered. My ancestor Ezekiel Cheever was part of the trials. He and his friend Cotton Mather helped to identify some of the witches— mostly feisty older women with their own property. The executions took place on the north side of town, a few minutes' walk from the Hathorne House. In order to bury them, their families had to remove their bodies in secret and prepare secret graves.

In the years since, many explanations have been put forward for what happened in Salem. Perhaps disease and famine and Indian raids had driven people mad with fear. Perhaps, as Arthur Miller hypothesized, the hysteria was started by a sexual young girl who had been having an illicit affair. Another theory, and this is the one which Hawthorne fleshed out in his *House of the Seven Gables,* is that the trials were a land grab targeting those whose property was coveted by the judges or whose land just seemed to cry out for transfer no matter what the cost. Salem still sometimes haunts me four centuries later, because of the evil that took hold of Ezekiel and the incalculable damage he did. Hawthorne was more severely haunted.

"If New England was socially a very small place in those days," wrote Henry James in his 1879 biography of Hawthorne, "Salem was a still smaller one; and if the American tone at large was intensely provincial, that of New England was not helped by having the best of it." What New England lacked in sophistication, Hawthorne was pushed to make up for in his imagination.

Hawthorne was raised in a prosperous family about to decline slowly in a prosperous town also on the brink of a fatal decline. When he was a boy, Salem was buzzing with trade; the Derby and Crowninshield wharves were a forest of masts, with sailing ships leaving and coming back every day from foreign ports with their exotic and luxurious cargoes of China tea, silks, and porcelains; Dutch gin and Jamaican rum; and their ballasts of blue and white export and Canton china, which decorated the federal houses of the great shipowners on Essex and Chestnut streets. Crowds of sailors from all ports and tradesmen with all kinds of wares crowded the streets around the wharves. Horses pulled heavy loads of strange cargoes through the streets.

In the house on Union Street where Hathorne was born, a kite string's length from the bustling wharves, the thriving surface was always hovering above a sharp consciousness of the town's evil history. Even as men bought and sold, married and had families, went to the Unitarian Church on the corner, and strolled on the Salem Green, they were everywhere reminded of what had happened in Salem and of the way an ugly wave can sweep through a community and turn neighbor against neighbor, brother against sister, mother against child.

In some ways, Nathaniel Hathorne was a typical nineteenth-century boy, petted by his sisters and packed off to a good college, but there seemed to be something in his nature that was sensitive to the complicated air of human affairs. At Bowdoin, he didn't do particularly well, although he made the acquaintance of Henry Wadsworth Longfellow and became a close friend of Horatio Bridge, a Maine law student who would be a lifelong friend, and of future President Franklin Pierce. Nothing seemed to fire him up, and a pleasant indecisiveness seems to have been part of his personality as a college student. After graduating from college and deciding to be a writer—he rejected the other possible professions of the ministry, the law, and medicine as too hard—Nathaniel Hawthorne moved back into his sister's house on Herbert Street in Salem, went up to his bedroom, and lived there for twelve years.

From his graduation in June of 1825 until the publication of *Twice-Told Tales* in 1837, Hawthorne spent most of his time in the upstairs bedroom of his family house. He came and went freely, going on some walking tours, but he seems to have been suffering from some kind of terminal introspection, schooling himself in the writers' life by reading and writing and rewriting and even completing a novel. On his limited inherited income, he thought this was the way to a writing career. But his short stories and an early novel, *Fanshawe,* as Rick Moody writes in his memoir *The Black Veil,* "didn't register even briefly in the national consciousness." Still he wrote.

In seclusion—and he and his sisters often even ate all their meals in their own rooms—Hawthorne produced a series of remarkable stories for a magazine called *The Token.* He made friends with Elizabeth

Peabody and kept up his Bowdoin friendships, but he rarely left his room except at night when a village bonfire or a public event might bring him out to lurk at the edges of the crowd and observe. "My brother goes out when there is a fire," his sister wrote.

For six months in 1836, he moved to Boston to produce the *American Magazine of Useful and Entertaining Knowledge* for a promised $500 a year. He wrote and edited almost the entire contents of the magazine. This gave him little time or money for anything other than writing and hardly improved on the reclusive life in Herbert Street, to which he returned with relief the next winter. Hawthorne's financial problems began to mount. His chosen profession paid little and late. Friends like Horatio Bridge worried and sent unsolicited checks. This combination of pittances from his writing and contributions from friends would barely be enough for Hawthorne to live on for the next decade and a half.

Eventually, in 1837, some good reviews—one from Henry Wadsworth Longfellow, no less—and the irresistible meddling of Elizabeth Palmer Peabody, who had liked his published work and insisted on the two families becoming friends, finally caused him to emerge from the bedroom of the house on Herbert Street, emotionally blinking as if it were his first experience of the light of day.

12

HAWTHORNE EMERGES

———◆———

Hawthorne didn't come out gradually. Suddenly, he wanted to do everything. A bachelor who his sister had predicted would never marry was immediately the subject of town gossip. He flamboyantly courted the gorgeous and rich Mary Silsbee and the garrulous and intellectual Elizabeth Peabody at the same time, finally settling after a wild year to everyone's surprise and some disappointment on Elizabeth's slight, invalid sister Sophia.

"In love quarrels a man goes off on stilts and comes back on his knees," Hawthorne noticed. But it was Elizabeth Peabody who seemed to end up on her knees in the matter of Hawthorne and the Peabody sisters. Hawthorne was deeply attracted to intelligent, even flamboyant women, and they to him. He loved nothing better than an intellectual engagement with someone of the opposite sex. In the end though, he often shied away from such women and turned toward more insipid conventional women who would be easy for him to handle. He was in love with challenge, but he didn't want to live with it. He courted Elizabeth and eventually proposed to her invalid sister Sophia. For many reasons, Hawthorne and Sophia decided to keep their new status a secret.

Hawthorne seemed to have been gathering force during all those solitary years as a recluse. He seemed to be replacing his ambivalence about his fellow human beings with an ability to juggle them so that he at least never felt overwhelmed. He didn't mind the Peabody sisters' being invited over to the Silsbees' grand house to see the new portrait of Mary Silsbee painted by Catherine Scollay, a portrait in which the glorious central female is pursued by a mysterious male huntsman with features and physique amazingly similar to Hawthorne's.

For a while, he took a job at the Salem Custom House working to inventory the merchandise that came into the docks and went out on the fewer and fewer remaining tall ships of the China trade. But he still wanted to go everywhere and do everything. Launched on a six-month tour toward the West, he got as far as Niagara Falls, and along the way lived in hotels by the side of the road, and spent a few months in North Adams, Massachusetts, just because he liked the way it looked.

In the meantime, dozens of communities were being planned and quite a few actually formed around Boston in a movement called associationism. This movement, based on the ideas of the French philosopher Charles Fourier, combined the fact of the United States' almost unlimited land with the idea that groups of men and women could live in harmony with nature and each other if only everything were properly planned. Uncomfortable with his secret engagement, and ready to leave his sisters' house but not really knowing where else to turn, Hawthorne took a dramatic step. He was one of the first and most unlikely subscribers to George Ripley's Brook Farm. He plunked down $1,000 and moved into the building called the Hive in West Roxbury in April of 1840.

At Brook Farm he hoped to write, but his chores, which at first seemed amusing, began to wear on him. He was in charge of shoveling the manure hill that farmers called "the Gold Mine." He learned to milk a cow. He joked about a new addition to the Brook Farm herd that belonged to Margaret Fuller, calling it the Transcendental heifer and noting that it was fractious and apt to kick over the milk pail. Brook Farm was beautiful, and in the summer it was fun to pretend to be farmers and ploughmen. Margaret Fuller came to spend the evening with the farmers, and with her long dark hair, held back with a bright flower, and her sharp, educated conversation, she had an electrifying effect.

Many Utopian experiments founded during the delicious New England spring and summer floundered during the cold, punishing winters. By November, Hawthorne was ready to leave Brook Farm and asked Ripley for a refund on his deposit. He hadn't gotten any work done, and he was tired of being cold all the time. Again,

Hawthorne seemed to have been storing up energy in the time when he wasn't writing. During the winter of 1841–42 he produced a series for children called *Grandfather's Chair* in which he told the history of a chair from the time it came to Massachusetts on the Puritan sailing ship the *Arbella,* the flagship of the Winthrop Fleet, to the present, and he produced a second volume of twice-told tales that was also well reviewed, this time by Edgar Allan Poe.

By June of 1842 after almost three years of engagement, Hawthorne and Sophia actually got ready to be married. Emerson hadn't been a great fan of Hawthorne's work—"Alcott and he together would make a man," he famously said—but he liked Sophia and was eager to add to his new community. The newlyweds would be moving into an old Emerson house, the Old Manse on the Concord River a stone's throw from the foundations of the Old North Bridge.

Eighteen forty-two had been a dreadful year in Concord. John Thoreau was dead by January 11, and Waldo Emerson had died on January 27. Lidian Emerson was devastated; Emerson was in mourning for his lost boy. Thoreau was locked in his own secret pain. Perhaps they thought the advent of the new couple would lighten their spirits.

Before even moving in, Sophia had tendered an invitation to her friend Margaret Fuller, whose "Conversations" delivered from a stage in Boston had mesmerized all who heard them. Sophia had been a disciple of Fuller's, and Fuller, who had met Hawthorne at Brook Farm and lived with him there, was very much in favor of Sophia's marriage. "If I ever saw a man who combined delicate tenderness to understand the heart of a woman with quiet depth and manliness enough to satisfy her it is Mr. Hawthorne," Fuller wrote prophetically. Instead of staying with the Hawthornes, where she would be witness to that quiet depth and manliness and understanding of the heart of woman every day, Fuller stayed with the Emersons, causing all kinds of passion, misunderstandings, and bitterness as the summer progressed.

13

THE EXECUTION

—◆—

The wedding of Nathaniel Hawthorne and Sophia Peabody took place in the Peabody parlor on West Street, after which Sophia and Hawthorne set out for Concord in a carriage. Hawthorne's sisters did not attend. "The execution took place yesterday," Hawthorne wrote his sister Louisa. "We made a Christian end and came straight to Paradise, where we abide at this present writing."

In the delicious discovery of individual importance, the seductions of nature, and the delights of European things among the group of people who gathered in Concord, there was a tremendous strain on all things conventional—and the institution of marriage was no exception. How could the men and women of the "newness" reconcile their desires for each other with an old-fashioned way of doing things that had been seemingly invented by the Puritans for their own protection? It wasn't just Hawthorne who compared marriage to execution. Emerson quoted Byron as saying that "the process of love to marriage is like wine to vinegar" and also liked to quote the British physician Thomas Wharton on marriage versus hanging: "Hanging is the better of the twayne / Sooner done and shorter payne." He liked Sir Thomas More's opinion that getting married is like putting one's hand in a bag containing "99 snakes and one eel."

Bronson Alcott, in his doomed consociate society, believed that marriage shouldn't limit a man's ability to be with other women or a woman's ability to be with other men, a freedom that rang hollow to his wife, who had no desire to be with other men and less and less desire to be with Alcott himself. Although Brook Farm didn't spell this out, most Utopian communities included some kind of implicit or explicit relief from the bonds of matrimony.

This new sexual and sensual freedom, whether physically expressed or suppressed, seems to have led to a level of complication in the Concord group. The Thoreau brothers both loved Ellen Sewall, and later, when he was living at the Emersons', Thoreau fell in love with Lidian Emerson after having done some flirting with her sister. Hawthorne courted both Peabody sisters, and after marrying Sophia was intensely involved with Margaret Fuller while she and Emerson were exchanging love letters. Louisa May Alcott seems to have been alternately in love with both Emerson—the intellectual—and Thoreau—the natural man—and this passionate dichotomy is the basis of her novel *Moods*.

After all, Emerson had questioned church doctrine and left the church. He had challenged Harvard and left the university. Both Thoreau and Alcott, his disciples, challenged the community so directly that they ended up headed for jail. These actions were all about reinventing the world outside of the old structures—and one of the oldest was marriage.

Although he loved Concord, and living with his obliging new wife in the Old Manse did seem like paradise, Hawthorne took a dim view of many of the self-appointed philosophers who gathered there. Shortly after the Hawthornes' arrival in Concord, Emerson and Thoreau paid a formal visit to the couple. It was not a success. Seated in the parlor, none of the three men ever got beyond the painful pleasantries of introduction. "Men do not after all meet on the ground of their real acquaintance and actual understanding of one another," Thoreau had written in his journal earlier that year, "but degrade themselves immediately into the puppets of convention." But in his notebooks, Hawthorne seemed to be thinking of Bronson Alcott and Jones Very when he wrote: "Never was a poor little country village infested with such a variety of queer, strangely-dressed, oddly behaved mortals, most of whom took themselves to be important agents of the world's destiny yet were simply bores of a very intense character."

Hawthorne slowly became friends with the other Concord writers, but he preferred silence. He spent hours fishing in the Assabet River above where it ran into the Concord with his friend Ellery Channing; he hiked through the woods with his neighbor Henry Thoreau. "Whatever question there may be of his talent, there can be none, I think, of his genius," wrote Henry James of Thoreau in his biography *Hawthorne*. Hawthorne and Thoreau eventually became close friends, going on paddling trips together and chatting about the natural world, talks in which Thoreau was the ultimate authority. Hawthorne told Thoreau stories of his own ancestors the Puritans, and Thoreau told Hawthorne stories of Concord's original settlers the Wampanoags, who had built a camp on the river behind the softly sloping hill where the Old Manse sat. "Thoreau, who has a strange faculty of finding what the Indians have left behind them, first set me on a search; and afterwards I enriched myself with some very perfect specimens," Hawthorne wrote of the arrowheads he found behind his house. "Their great charm consists in the rudeness and in the individuality of each article." Hawthorne and Sophia were always running out of money; poverty was a virtue among these men and women, but it was also an inconvenience.

Hawthorne and Emerson, on the other hand, never really liked each other. Emerson thought Hawthorne's writing too much about the past. Hawthorne thought Emerson too much of the Great Man about Concord. "For myself there had been epochs of my life when I, too, might have asked of this prophet the master word that should solve me the riddle of the universe," Hawthorne jibed, "but now, being happy, I felt as if there were no question to be put." The lack of attraction between Hawthorne and Emerson might have been easily absorbed by their mutual friends and their love of books, but whatever had gone wrong between them from the beginning was made much, much worse by the presence of the woman with whom they both became erotically and imaginatively entangled.

Sophia already adored Margaret Fuller, so much that Hawthorne had worried about her influence on the tender mind of his fiancée. He didn't like the idea that Sophia would come under the power of others, and was deeply upset when his young bride-to-be wanted to experiment with mesmerism and phrenology. The summer the Hawthornes moved to Concord, Margaret Fuller was staying at the Emersons', in a family shattered by grief. While Lidian Emerson stayed upstairs,

Fuller and Emerson took long, healing walks, walks that clearly seemed to Fuller to involve more than intellectual companionship. Soon, Fuller began walking across town to the Old Manse to see the Hawthornes, and her old admiration for Hawthorne was rekindled. Emerson was furiously jealous.

14

ANOTHER TRIANGLE

———◆———

One afternoon in August, Hawthorne and Sophia were interrupted by a surprise visit from Margaret Fuller, who had walked across town—a distance of more than a mile—in the dreamy afternoon light. After she stayed for tea and conversation Hawthorne walked Fuller back to the Emerson House. They walked side by side in the moonlight, down the road to town and past the monument and out of town on the Lexington Road and down to the Cambridge Turnpike. As they talked, Fuller reached out to touch his arm when she made a point, and the electricity between them seemed to generate sparks in the dark. Fuller had left a book behind at the Old Manse, and the next day Hawthorne returned it to the Emerson House.

He dropped the book off without calling, and on his way home he happened to run into Margaret lying beside the wooded pathway reading a book. Was it a chance meeting? It was a happy one. He sat down beside her on the moss and looked up ecstatically at the summer trees. Other walkers passed by, smiling at these two people engrossed in their murmuring intimate conversation. "What a happy, happy day," Fuller wrote later. Hawthorne and Fuller, sheltered by the woods, watched a few thrushes chase each other and a butterfly lazily flit past near a bunch of wild red columbine. "Then we talked about Autumn—and about the pleasures of getting lost in the woods—and about the crows, whose voices Margaret had heard—and about the experiences of early childhood, whose influence remains upon the character after the recollection of them has passed away—and about the sight of mountains from a distance, and the view from their summits—and about other matters of high and low philosophy."

Suddenly, a shout interrupted the low conversation, and Emerson appeared in the woods, obviously looking for Margaret, but with a long story about searching for the Muses among the trees. He collected Margaret and took her back to his house, while Hawthorne wandered dreamily home and took a cooling moonlight swim in the slow-flowing Concord. Margaret stayed in Concord during the entire month of August that year, challenging Emerson romantically so completely that in the end she had to reassure him that she had no designs on the sanctity of his marriage. The nature of their friendship, sometimes erotic, sometimes romantic, sometimes intellectual, was the subject of Emerson's essay "Friendship." The Yankee Plato, as Alcott called him, having suffered the loss of brothers, his first wife, and then his son Waldo, was not about to give up the island of serenity and stability he had finally established in the white house on the Cambridge Turnpike. Nevertheless, he was restless.

Both Hawthorne and Emerson had known Fuller for a few years. She and Hawthorne had done the chores and milked the cows together at Brook Farm, and she had edited Emerson's magazine, but she continued to surprise them with her erudition and passion. At a time when women were prized for their obedience, Fuller had a habit of skewering pretension with wit. She was a Dorothy Parker woman in a Jane Austen world. In fact, her acquaintance Edgar Allan Poe divided people into three types: men, women, and Margaret Fuller.

Growing up in Cambridgeport, Massachusetts, Fuller was educated by her distinguished congressman father. She was tutored in Latin, Greek, and German, and read Tacitus, Virgil, and Goethe. She had a quick mind to go with her erudition. "Mediocrity is obscurity," her father said, and with her fast conversation and flashing eyes in a plain but animated face, she cut a wide swath through the Harvard community at a time when women didn't go to college. She was the first woman to be permitted to use the sacred Harvard Library. She worked for a winter for Bronson Alcott at the Temple School, which left her exhausted. Lidian Emerson was away, so Fuller's friend Emerson came to get her in a carriage and together they drove back to Concord in the spring weather. In Concord on this visit and her subsequent frequent visits, she made a vivid impression.

In the morning, she and Emerson would read and write in their respective rooms, she in her study and bedroom and he across the hall in his study. "Then he reads to me, or we talk the remaining hours." Fuller is an inspiration for Hester Prynne in Hawthorne's *The Scarlet Letter,* which draws on Fuller's book *Woman in the Nineteenth Century* for its polemical chapters, on Hawthorne's experience with Margaret in the woods for its most romantic chapter, and on Margaret's later circumstances for much of its premise. Fuller is also a model for Henry James and James Russell Lowell heroines.

Fuller's work and her life were so affecting because she was dedicated to a revolution on behalf of women in society. Her personal anti-slavery campaign was supported by her actions and the way she lived her own life, with what was then a shocking degree of independence for a woman. She made her living giving "Conversations" at a time when it was illegal for a woman to do public speaking for pay. She lived alone and spurned the idea of marriage at a time when marriage was the only alternative to a long, bleak spinsterhood in most women's minds. She took the kinds of jobs that only men had before her. Caught between her own energy and intelligence and the inhibitions of her community, she sometimes seems tragic, sometimes farcical. When she was offered the editorship of the *New York Tribune* by Horace Greeley, she couldn't take the job until she had found a respectable family with whom to board—young women didn't live alone in the 1840s no matter who they were.

Although written in old-fashioned language, her principal surviving work, which began as an essay in *The Dial* titled "The Great Lawsuit: Man versus Men, Woman versus Women," lays out the foundations of modern feminism. At a time when women were almost as disenfranchised and enslaved as those owned in actual slavery, Fuller's protestations were revolutionary, and even today they have the awful ring of truth. "Early I perceived that men, never in any extreme of despair, wished to be women," she writes in a direct plea for the kinds of freedom—freedom in work and in life—that were taken for granted by men. Although the turgid, quotation-ridden prose certainly slowed the spread of her ideas, some of them would still be original today. "Freedom and equality have been proclaimed only to leave room for a monstrous display of slave-dealing and slave-keeping; though the free American often feels himself free, like the Roman, only to pamper his appetites and indolence through the misery of his fellow beings, still it is not in vain, that the verbal statement has been made, 'All men are born free and equal,' " she writes. But what about women?

For all the modernism of Fuller's ideas, the 1840s were another age—many ages from our own. Even as Bronson Alcott believed that blondness equaled goodness, and a craze for mesmerism and spiritual quackery and phrenology swept New England, sailors landing on the Pacific Islands believed that—without question—the islanders would be better off as converted Christians than as they were, living in their island paradise. People still believed that at the north and south poles the globe was indented with a tropical paradise. Another of the exotic beliefs of the age was that women were inferior to men.

This state of affairs offered at least two alternatives to women who lived long enough to have the choice. They could pretend weakness and adoring submission as Sophia Hawthorne did and live their lives behind the protective mask of marriage. Or they could own up to their intellectual strength and ability to learn as Margaret Fuller did, and know that all the men they fell in and out of love with would be married or would marry other kinds of women. The time came when Margaret Fuller had to tell Emerson that she could no longer edit his magazine, *The Dial,* without getting paid for it as he had clearly expected her to do. The salary of $200 a year had never been forthcoming. Emerson took over the editorship and Fuller moved on.

Part Two

15

BRONSON ALCOTT, PEDDLER
TURNED PEDANT

—◆—

Much of the world was unmapped in the first half of the nineteenth century. Captain Charles Wilkes had set off on the great United States Exploring Expedition to circumnavigate the globe and bring back as many species of plants and animals as he could find. Nature seemed to have unlimited abundance. Most British and American travelers still believed in their own superiority and thought they were doing the natives a favor by acquainting them with the "true," Western way of living.

This confidence was at its height in New England, where the great issues were constantly debated, where every storekeeper and teacher was a small-town Plato, and where most people were certain that what they believed was right; they believed that slavery was wrong, that no one should be judged by the color of their skin, and that rumblings from the southern states were nothing more than greed, discontent, and a reluctance to do the right thing.

Bronson Alcott was very much a man of his times, a man whose idealism had served him well. What served him was not always what would serve his wife and four daughters. Long before Henry David Thoreau was famously arrested for not paying taxes, his neighbor Alcott had quit paying his and would happily have gone to jail if a neighbor (not Ralph Waldo Emerson for once) had not stepped in and paid off his debt.

When Thoreau finally managed to get himself arrested for refusing to pay taxes in a country that supported slavery, he was elated. The jailer, Sam Staples, was a friend, who offered to pay the tax himself. Thoreau refused. Then his Aunt Maria showed up and paid the tax, but by that time Sam Staples had decided to do his friend a favor and go home for the night. Not only did Thoreau get to chat with the other prisoners, but he had an exchange with Emerson that has become a watchword for civil disobedience. Emerson, visiting during the few hours Thoreau was incarcerated, is said to have asked "What are you doing in there?" to which the indigent and intransigent Thoreau replied, "What are you doing out there?"

Born in unpleasant circumstances on a farm in northern Connecticut, Alcott fancied himself an educational philosopher even as a schoolboy. When his schooling ended at the age of thirteen, he imagined becoming a schoolteacher, but his lack of qualifications made that impossible. He was charming, he was a great talker, he was handsome and charismatic, but he did not even have a high school diploma. Later, in Concord as a member of a variety of conversation clubs formed by Emerson, Bronson Alcott was often the only man who hadn't gone to college in a group of men who had gone to Harvard and taught at Harvard. In these circumstances, he liked to claim that this lack of formal education was an asset and nurtured his ability to think freely.

As a young man, after being disappointed in not finding a way to teach, Alcott headed south to become a successful traveling peddler. With his melodious voice and blazing blue eyes, he sold combs, sewing notions, and fabrics to the gentlewomen of the Tidewater, and this was where he got his real education. He saw the freedom of the wealthy and decided to adopt it for himself, whether or not he was actually wealthy. His experience in the homes of the southern gentry caused him to change his name from Amos Alcox to the more pompous and important sounding A. Bronson Alcott and to change his manner to that of an aristocrat too fine for anything as mundane as financial responsibility. As Geraldine Brooks suggests in her novel *March* on the subject of Alcott's adventures in the South as a peddler, his time in Virginia and the Carolinas was a sexual as well as a political education.

Alcott remained a strange mixture of beliefs. He thought that his daughter Louisa was naughty because of her dark eyes and hair. At the same time, he sheltered runaway slaves in his house, which became a stop on the Underground Railroad to Canada, and he founded Boston's first white antislavery society.

In the contest between Alcott's pretension and his charismatic idealism, his pretension often won. Alcott's writing is almost impenetrable, but in person he was a quick-witted man whose uncompromising view of the world and of education earned him many friends and followers, including Ralph Waldo Emerson. "His discourse soars to a wonderful height, so regular, so lucid, so playful, so new and disdainful of all boundaries of tradition and experience," wrote Emerson soon after Alcott moved his family to Concord. William Ellery Channing, taking in his agrarian philosophy and his orphic discourse, dubbed Alcott, the former traveling salesman, Orpheus at the Plough; Alcott's Greek was always rusty. His writing sometimes seems to use ornate pedantry to make up for his lack of education.

Discouraged by what he perceived as a lukewarm reception in Concord—there were no crowds of students or cries of recognition when he walked through town—Alcott found out that a group of Englishmen and women had become enchanted by his teachings and had opened a school named after him in Surrey, England, in a village called Ham Common. At this British Alcott house, his book on education, the infamous *Conversations with Children on the Gospels,* was treated as a sacred text. The very book that had been called an indecent and obscene book by the *Courier* of Boston for its discussion of procreation, and which had indirectly caused Alcott to lose his last few pupils and have to shut down his beloved Temple School, had finally found an appreciative audience. Except for Emerson and the loyal Elizabeth Peabody, no one else seemed to understand his great book. At least Emerson defended him. "I hate to have all the little dogs barking at you," he had written after the book was attacked. "For you have something better to do than attend to them: but every beast must do after its kind, & why not these."

Now it turned out that his true followers had been in England all along. Alcott must go! With a ticket paid for by Emerson, Alcott left for Surrey, abandoning his wife and four girls to make do in the Hosmer cottage which at least now boasted a robust garden that Alcott had grown with the help of his friend Thoreau. In Surrey, Alcott was shown around the kingdom by a British financial journalist who worked as the head of the school. The school was a great success, and the journalist, Charles Lane, persuaded Alcott to think about founding a true Alcottian community, a "second Eden" where children could be educated as if their interests were important, and men and women could live in harmony.

Although Alcott had had nothing but disdain for other communities that had grown up with similar ideas around Concord—specifically Brook Farm—he embraced the idea of a "consociate community" founded on his own philosophies. After all, Lane had the cash.

Back in Concord, Lane, his son, and another teacher, named Henry Wright, all squeezed into the small Alcott cottage—to the family's displeasure. Shopping for the location of the new paradise on earth, Lane picked out a dilapidated farmhouse on Prospect Hill surrounded by a split-rail fence near Harvard, Massachusetts, fourteen miles northwest of Concord.

In spite of Alcott's belief that private property was wrong, a belief he expressed at every opportunity, Lane paid $1,800 for the house and 100 acres. He wasn't buying the land, he told people, and he was redeeming it for "divine uses." They would be yielding their individual rights to the "Supreme Owner." Why Harvard, almost a day's travel from Concord? Perhaps Lane felt that Emerson had a bad influence on Alcott. Maybe he wanted their experiment to be free of Emerson's persuasive ideas and even more persuasive money.

16

FRUITLANDS

In 1843, Alcott and Lane began the "consociate" community in which their ideas could be put to the test. The Alcotts moved once again. On a cool day in June, the family was loaded into a horse-drawn wagon piled high with possessions, a few agricultural supplies, and Alcott's bust of Socrates. Alcott was elated. "We have made an arrangement with the proprietor of an estate of about a hundred acres, which liberates this tract from human ownership," he wrote in *The Dial*. "For picturesque beauty both in the near and far landscape, the spot has few rivals. A semi-circle of undulating hills stretches from south to west, among which the Wachusett and Monadnock are conspicuous. The vale, through which flows a tributary to the Nashua, is esteemed for its fertility and ease of cultivation."

There was a different point of view walking next to the horse-drawn wagon in a long homemade dress and bonnet. "The wind whistled over the bleak hills; the rain fell in a despondent drizzle, and twilight began to fall," wrote Louisa May Alcott, who at the age of ten was already considerably more adult and more observant than her dreamy father as the family moved out on this great mystic adventure. Later in life when she was rich and successful and could write what she wanted, she made fun of the whole thing in her short 1873 memoir *Transcendental Wild Oats*.

"But the calm man gazed as tranquilly into the fog as if he beheld a bow of promise spanning the gray sky," she wrote. "The cheery woman tried to cover everyone but herself with the big umbrella. The brown boy pillowed his head on the pate of Socrates and slumbered peacefully. The little girls sang lullabies to their dolls in soft, maternal murmurs. The sharp-nosed pedestrian marched steadily on, with the blue cloak streaming out behind him like a banner. . . ." In her sardonic look backward, Louisa referred to her father's dream house as "Apple Slump."

Louisa's recently discovered journals written during the Alcott family's months at Fruitlands show a young girl who tempers her optimism with a fierce acknowledgment of the realities of living without even the modest comforts the Alcotts had come to take for granted. All four girls slept in an attic bedroom under the roof, where the rain made a lovely sound on the boards—and sometimes leaked in on the occupants. Under the eaves the heat gathered in the corners and the cold, when it came, seemed to ease right through. Alcott shared the popular belief in the curative powers of cold water. Many thought that whatever ailed them could be frozen out by icy baths, and sometimes ice was broken on the surface of the tub to make the morning ablutions. "I rose at five and had my bath. I love cold water! Then we had our singing lesson with Mr. Lane," Louisa wrote in her journal. "After breakfast I washed dishes and ran on the hill till nine and had some thoughts—it was so beautiful up there. . . . Father asked us what was God's noblest work. Anna said *men*, but I said *babies*. Men are often bad; babies never are. We had a long talk, and I felt better after it, and *cleared up*. . . . We had bread and fruit for dinner."

At Fruitlands, Bronson Alcott's ideas grew to their looniest ripeness, although little else that was planted there ever had a chance. Alcott's ideas prohibited any exploitation of animals—cows were not to be robbed of their milk, nor horses of their manure for fertilizer, nor chickens of their eggs, nor sheep of their wool. Animals would not be exploited by being yoked and forced to drive a plough. There would be no theft of honey from the bees, nor stealing of their wax. Dressed in floppy brown linen and living by the light of candles, the family and their hangers-on were to eat unleavened bread, porridge, and water for breakfast; bread, vegetables, and water for lunch; and bread, fruit, and water for supper. Without manure or the use of animals for farming, the little community was doomed to fail at growing and making their own food, Alcott's Edenic ideal.

A group of assorted people who didn't seem to fit in anywhere else in the whole wide world moved into Fruitlands with the Alcott family, including a refugee from Brook Farm named Isaac Hecker who had been part owner in a New York banking firm and who had become unable to cope with daily life because of nervous fits and hearing imaginary voices. He later became a Roman Catholic priest. "A second irrepressible being held that all the emotions of the soul should be freely expressed," wrote Louisa May Alcott in *Transcendental Wild Oats.* "And illustrated his theory by antics that would have sent him to a lunatic asylum, if, as an unregenerate wag said, he had not already been in one. When his spirit soared, he climbed trees and shouted; when doubt assailed him, he lay upon the floor and groaned lamentably."

Another member of the consociate society was Abraham Everett, who renamed himself Wood Abram. Samuel Bower, a British member, insisted on his right to go nude, while Samuel Larned came from a group of intellectuals in Providence, Rhode Island, who had admired the Transcendentalists from afar. Close up, Larned was less than admiring. The only woman besides Mrs. Alcott, a writer of poetry named Ann Page, was expelled during the first few days for eating a piece of fish, presumably without its express permission.

"Are there any beasts of burden on the place?" Louisa has Ann Page disguised as "Jane Page" ask in *Transcendental Wild Oats.* "Only one woman!" answered Abba Alcott.

"Unfortunately the poor lady hankered after the fleshpots, and endeavored to stay herself with private sips of milk, crackers and cheese, and on one dire occasion she partook of fish at a neighbor's table," Louisa writes of the unfortunate Page. "One of the children reported this sad lapse, and poor Jane was publicly reprimanded.

"'I only took a little bit of the tail,' sobbed the penitent poetess.

"'Yes, but the whole fish had to be tortured and slain that you might tempt your carnal appetite with that one taste of tail. Know ye not, consumers of flesh meat, that ye are nourishing the wolf and tiger in your bosoms?'" exclaimed the outraged leader. There were always second helpings of outrage at Fruitlands. Ann Page left the room in tears, packed her belongings, and left.

Another Fruitlands recruit was Joseph Palmer, who later bought the property from Lane—who unliberated it for a price—and then ran it as a kind of refuge for anyone who wanted to live there. Palmer was a bearded man who had been persecuted for his insistence on growing and maintaining his superfluous facial hair. He had been beaten up, had his beard cut off, and he had even been thrown in prison.

Although Fruitlands was based on the idea of the evils of property, most of its residents had some. Palmer in fact owned a large tract of land and ran a butchering business in Fitchburg. He occasionally had to leave the colony where cows were treated like honored friends to tend to his cattle who were not so lucky. "The entrance to paradise is still through the strait and narrow gate of self-denial," Alcott wrote just before heading to Fruitlands. "Eden's Avenue is yet guarded by fiery-sworded cherubim, and humility and charity are the credentials for admission." These men had plenty of ideas, and perhaps some humility and charity as well, but none of them seemed to have any of the physical skills necessary for survival on a plot of land in New England.

Thoreau, always a good friend of Alcott's, was comfortably indispensable at the Emersons' and furthermore had no money to contribute. That was his excuse for not joining the family at Fruitlands. In many ways, he understood Alcott's idealism of the unlettered man, the man who hadn't gone to Harvard and couldn't read German or even Greek. "I have often been astonished at the force and precision of style to which busy laboring men, unpracticed in writing, easily attain when they are required to make the effort," he wrote in his journals around the time Alcott returned from England. "The scholar not infrequently envies the propriety and emphasis with which the farmer calls to his team, and confesses that if that lingo were written it would surpass his labored sentences."

For a while, the experiment seemed to be going well in spite of the fact that at harvest time, Bronson Alcott and Charles Lane were too busy preaching to have anything to do with the crops. "They look well in July," wrote Emerson prophetically, "we will see them in December." They admired the neighboring Shakers but couldn't reproduce their discipline.

In each of the Utopian communities that sprang up in these years, there were many rules and regulations installed to create the "freedom" usually promised by the community elders, and Fruitlands was no exception. In most of these communities, sex was regarded as a portion of the lowly physical part of human endeavor. In some, it was practiced completely without regulations—the freedom was direct.

Most of these communities were based more or less on the Fourier-ian theory that society had to be rebuilt from scratch. Fourier believed in the goodness of human nature. If people were free to do what they wanted, to follow what Fourier called their "passions," they would automatically live in love and harmony, he wrote. Communities or "phalanxes" of 1,620 members should come together and garden, per-form, and have sex to their heart's content, he thought. This would insure peace on earth. None of the communities in the New England "associationist" movement ever approached 1,620 members, but many of Fourier's ideas were employed nevertheless.

Bronson never seems to have decided exactly what role sex should play in his consociate society, although he personally felt the need for a physical freedom to match his spiritual freedom. He spoke to his wife and children about breaking up their family if they could not accept his philosophy. At other times—and his sojourn at Fruitlands appears to have been one of them—he decided to renounce sex altogether.

Abba Alcott went along with most of her husband's eccentric ideas and added a few wild ones of her own. She was a follower of Dr. Sylvester Graham, who believed that American men were suffering from a variety of illnesses, including weakened brains and lungs because of the loss of semen during sexual activity, according to Martha Saxton's biography of Louisa, *Louisa May.* According to Graham, an ounce of lost semen was the equivalent of forty ounces of blood. After four difficult births, it's hard to imagine that Abba Alcott was disappointed at her hus-band's striving for celibacy, but she was. Charles Lane, however, found himself drawn to the Shaker ideal of complete celibacy.

17

SEX

◆

Sexual mores were changing from the more liberal ways of the eighteenth century to the uptight views of the American Victorians after the Civil War. In the 1840s, it was not permitted for women to enjoy sex, but in the Transcendental world of bohemian life with financing often tenuous and poverty haunting everything, sexual favors seem to have sometimes been bartered for security. In the years after the American Revolution, a freer sexual morality—more of a frontier morality—seemed to prevail. As a girl, Eliza watched her mother sexually give in to a man named Royall Tyler. Tyler, who also had a relationship with John and Abigail Adams's older daughter Nabby and broke her heart, would later become famous as America's first playwright with his comedy of manners titled *The Contrast*.

According to Megan Marshall's biography *The Peabody Sisters,* Tyler was a boarder whom Betsey Peabody took into their house on School Street in Boston. Tyler did more than help cover expenses, but the family paid a high price for his help. Elizabeth Peabody later referred to him as a polluted wretch "who enters a worthy family and leaves it not, till some victim falls prey to his designs." After sleeping with Eliza's mother, Tyler also molested Eliza and her sister Mary, and the Peabody sisters all knew that their sister Sophia was in fact Royall's daughter.

It's an anomaly of history that societies in which sex is openly discussed are not necessarily societies in which sex is rampant. Recently, for instance, as sexual explicitness has exploded on our televisions and in our magazines and books, teenage pregnancies have actually dropped. The Transcendentalists never talked about sex. Reading their work would give the impression that they were much more interested in religion or in nature than they were in sex. There are clues that this was not the case. Hawthorne in *The Scarlet Letter* wrote a brilliant novel about sex—sex with a woman much like Margaret Fuller. His story of love, secrets, revenge, and betrayal is wrapped around the dark character of a spurned older man and a woman who bears an illegitimate child.

Hawthorne was obviously very aware of the power of sex to ruin lives, as it does in *The Scarlet Letter.* But he was also aware of its joys and its amazing connections. He understood the thrills and guilts of sexual relationships that were conducted outside of marriage, conducted in a private world well insulated from the town elders or governors. The tenderest scene in the book, set in the woods where the crows are calling, is between the two separated lovers as they recall the pleasure of sexual relationship for which Hester has been ordered to wear a scarlet *A* and Arthur Dimmesdale has been forced to keep a secret which eventually kills him.

"What we did had a consecration of its own," Hester says to her former lover as they sit together. She has been punished but not chastened. "We felt it so! We said so to each other! Hast thou forgotten it?"

"'Hush, Hester,' said Arthur Dimmesdale, rising from the ground. 'No: I have not forgotten!' "

American marriage in the century before Bronson Alcott had been a convenient, short-lived affair, useful for building homesteads, starting families, and doing the backbreaking work of colonizing the American wilderness. Now, for the first time, men like Alcott and George Ripley were trying to redefine marriage, to create an institution that would have a spiritual dimension as well as physical and legal ones. Marriage was becoming less and less a practical matter and more and more a matter of enjoyment, or at least companionship.

Both of Emerson's marriages were imminently practical, as was Alcott's and even, in its own way, Hawthorne's. Each man chose a woman who would help him financially or emotionally or both. Still, all these men were also modern enough to think of their needs outside of marriage as important.

Lane was disturbed by the physical dimension of sex and felt that Alcott could never reach a higher level of spiritual development because of his insistence on having it. Perhaps Lane was in love with Alcott himself. At any rate, he found the Shakers' way of life very appealing. He was also cold and hungry at Fruitlands. They should all join the Shakers, Lane announced. Abba Alcott did not want to join the Shakers, a move which she rightly felt would spell the end of her little family of girls. Lane accused her of selfishness. She held her ground. By the end of the winter of 1844, Lane had taken his son and his money and left the farmhouse in Harvard to join the nearby Shaker village.

The collapse of Fruitlands sent Alcott to bed in a depression. He became a "wan shadow of a man," according to Louisa, whose journal of her time at Fruitlands is mostly about playing horse in the woods and quarreling with her sisters. Abba Alcott quietly sold the family possessions and made a plan to move to rented rooms nearby. Bronson was forced to go along, even as she had been more or less forced to move to Fruitlands. The shift in power in the Alcott family that happened that winter became permanent. "So one bleak December day with their few possessions piled on top of an ox-sled, the rosy children perched atop, and the parents trudging arm in arm behind, the exiles left their Eden and faced the world again," concluded Louisa with irony in *Transcendental Wild Oats*. By 1845, the family was back in Concord.

18

THOREAU GOES TO
NEW YORK CITY

———◆———

As the lives of these men and women unfolded in the sleepy precincts of Concord, the world moved on. *The Dial,* the magazine that had been the manifestation of Emerson's friendship with Margaret Fuller and which had published Thoreau as well, finally folded. A sailor named Herman Melville got paid off at the Boston Navy Yard after four years at sea on the whaling ship the *Acushnet,* and on the *Lucy Ann,* the *Charles & Henry,* and the *United States.* He was warmly welcomed home by his family and started writing a book about his experiences titled *Typee.* In the U.S. House of Representatives, the elder statesman and former President John Quincy Adams carried the vote for repeal of a gag rule against discussions of slavery. Although Adams would agree with Emerson on that subject, he was one of the critics of the controversial writer. "A young man named Ralph Waldo Emerson, a son of my once-loved friend William Emerson," wrote Adams in 1840, "after failing in the avocations of a Unitarian preacher and school-master, starts a new doctrine of Transcendentalism, declares all the old revelations superannuated and worn out, and announces the approach of new revelations."

In the summer of 1844, the Fitchburg Railroad, which ran between Boston and Fitchburg to the northwest of Concord, opened its tracks, cutting the traveling time between Concord and Boston from more than three hours on an expensive coach with horses to an hour's ride costing fifty cents. Lounging on the grass under the oaks and maples at

Sleepy Hollow, where he and Margaret had so recently discussed crows and other things, Hawthorne heard the first train whistle one idle July afternoon. He knew what it meant. "It brings the noisy world into the midst of our slumberous peace," he wrote.

Was Henry David Thoreau a Renaissance man, a prophet without much honor in his own little town, or was he a bum mooching off of his friends when his own family got tired of him? Was he the courageous man who ferried runaway slaves into Canada, often buying their train tickets and driving them to the station? Or was he a loner who didn't care about anyone but himself? Sometimes it seemed as if Thoreau cared less about the human world than the animal world, about the spider mites on the mushrooms and the earthworms burrowing in the loamy soil, the nine-spotted ladybugs who flew in through the windows in the spring and who liked to drink sugar water, and the centipedes crouching under the fallen acorns around the big oaks on the Milldam. "I am a schoolmaster—a Private surveyor—a Gardener, a Farmer—a Painter, a housepainter, a Carpenter, a Mason, a Day Laborer and Pencil maker, a Glass-paper maker, a writer and sometimes a poetaster," Thoreau wrote to the secretary of his Harvard class.

By 1843, he had been living as the Emersons' friend and houseman for two years. Because he was tired of having Thoreau as a boarder, and also perhaps because he was concerned about his young friend's career, Emerson wrote to his cousin William Emerson, who lived on Staten Island, New York, asking if he needed a tutor for his children. Thoreau got the job. He set off with the idea that he could publish in New York, meet Walt Whitman and Edgar Allan Poe, both friends of Emerson's, and make some connections in the New York literary community.

New York was not to be Thoreau's place. Among the many people he met, few really interested him. He almost immediately longed for the life he had so casually given up. "I can remember when I was more enriched by a few cheap rays of light falling on the pond-side than by this broad sunny day," he had written. "Riches have wings indeed. The weight of present woe will express the sweetness of past experience. When sorrow comes, how easy it is to remember pleasure!" One man who interested Thoreau in spite of his homesickness was Horace Greeley, a New Hampshire native who, at the age of thirty-three, had founded the *New York Tribune*.

In spite of his new life and the stimulation of the city, he missed

Lidian Emerson dreadfully. The William Emersons were boring, and tutoring didn't inspire Thoreau as teaching had—at least, teaching in Concord. He was homesick for Concord, for his friends and family, for the rivers and the silence of his boat floating down the current, and for the beauty of the trees bowing down over the pastures. He wrote Lidian a frank letter of friendship bordering on something else. "You must know that you represent to me woman." He was devastated when she wrote back a cool note, a Dear Henry letter stressing their friendship. She did not miss him in the same way that he missed her.

Although he was able to write two pieces in New York and one, "A Winter Walk," showed that he was beginning to develop his mature writing style, his literary ambitions were frustrated. The only thing he managed to publish during his eight-month stay was a long review of Utopian J. A. Etzler's book entitled *The Paradise Within the Reach of All Men*. Thoreau didn't much like Etzler's scheme or anything else in New York. Within a few months, he was back at home, this time staying with his parents in the house on Parkman Street and making himself useful by helping with the pencil factory in the sheds behind the house.

To the accompaniment of the thump of the machines that stamped out wooden halves of pencils, filled them with the plumbago lead, and glued them together, Thoreau puzzled over a way to make a better pencil. Never satisfied with what easily presented itself, the young Thoreau experimented as the machines did their work. Would a drilled hole for the plumbago make a better pencil? Was there a way to design a better machine for the manufacture of the plumbago? He bought the best pencils sold in Boston and took them apart. Where did the Faber pencil get its durability? How did the French pencils keep their cylinder whole? As he worked, he breathed in the potent mix of lead and fine sawdust that would ultimately cloud his lungs. He was home, but he did not feel at all at home.

19

WALL OF FIRE

———◆———

Some days, as a respite from the pencil factory, Thoreau helped his father on various renovation and building projects in town, picking up a set of building skills that would later come in very handy. The Thoreaus had just bought a lot on Texas Street northwest of the center of town to build their first house—their homes, including the Parkman House, which is now the Concord Free Public Library, had always been rented. Thoreau spent days helping his father build from scratch, digging the cellar hole and pressing stones and mortar into its earthen walls, building the frame and raising it, and constructing the roof and windows. He was learning to build a house, but he wasn't writing at all. The problem was that if he did physical labor all day, he was unable to study or write at night. For the moment, he was less a writer than a handyman. On a walking trip through the Catskills with his friend Ellery Channing, Thoreau confided his frustration and his hopelessness. Things just got worse.

On a windy April day in 1844, Thoreau and another friend, the banker's son Edward Hoar, a Harvard senior from one of Concord's first families, paddled up the Sudbury River. They were headed for Fairhaven Bay, a widening of the river almost the size of a pond just a bit farther south of town than Walden Pond. Hoar was home from college on a few days' vacation, and Thoreau was taking the day off from working on pencils and the new house. Hoar worshiped Thoreau. When Hoar's parents had refused to let him have a gun, Thoreau had taken him hunting in the woods with his own single-barreled flintlock.

Rowing up the Sudbury between green banks, the two men passed by a crescent beach above the South Bridge and passed under the stone arches of the bridge, which carried the road west from Concord, and the new railroad bridge, which was bringing the Fitchburg line rails through town on the way from Boston.

On their way up the river, as they established a rhythm of stroking together, they made a few stops to fish. Thoreau was always a lucky fisherman, and by lunchtime they had caught enough to make a substantial meal. They stopped and pulled the boat up onto the shore. There they carefully built a cooking fire in a decaying old pine tree stump on the shores of Fairhaven Bay. At first, the fire didn't catch, and then suddenly it was out of control. The wind was more forceful than Thoreau had realized. To his great horror, the man who often felt at one with the forces of nature watched as his cooking fire grew wildly, burning off the dead wood of the stump and suddenly leaping onto the dry grass as if it had a life of its own. It had been a dry spring with little rain, and now the piney ground cover and the bushes seemed to instantaneously combust.

When it was clear that all the river water they could carry was useless, the two men started to go for help, Thoreau on foot and Hoar in the boat. After trying to interest one uninterested farmer, Thoreau finally got help, but turning to see a half-mile wall of flame, and realizing there was nothing else he could do, he walked to the cliffs above Fairhaven Bay to watch as the alarm bells rang and crowds finally arrived to put out the fire. By the time the blaze had been controlled and burned itself out, more than 300 acres of Concord woods and pastures had been demolished and Thoreau himself had become one of the least popular men in a town that always suspected him of being a little worse than strange.

The local paper, the *Concord Freeman,* condemned Thoreau and Hoar as "thoughtless and careless." Hoar's father paid damages to two families who had lost their woods, and there was also talk of prosecuting the two men for the damage done. It was six years before Thoreau could bring himself to write about it in his own journal. "I had felt like a guilty person,—nothing but shame and regret." Everyone knew that the young Hoar was not really to blame—hadn't he always been a student of Thoreau's? "I thank God for sorrow," Thoreau wrote in his journal that month. "It is hard to be abused. Is not He kind still who lets this south wind blow, this warm sun shine on me?"

In Washington that year, the Whigs nominated Henry Clay, the Democrats James Polk, and the news was carried by Morse's telegraph. Polk won the election. In 1845, Texas became the twenty-eighth state in the Union. It didn't matter much; to the thinkers in Concord, politics was still a distant rumble, punctuated by whatever they could do to oppose the horror of slavery. They were more excited about Edgar Allan Poe's publication of his long poem "The Raven." William Miller, who had founded the Millerite sect, predicted October 23 as the day the world would end, and the Millerites crowded the local hillsides dressed in white robes. They waited in vain.

Emerson would once again provide the solution for his indigent, inconvenient friend Thoreau. One morning in September 1844, Emerson took his morning walk to Walden Pond and ran into two men who were discussing the sale of a field on the shore. For $89.10 Emerson bought it. When a few friends came out to visit it later in the week— probably including Thoreau—he was persuaded to buy Heartwell Bigelow's pine grove next to it. Emerson was delighted with his new property and kept a journal about its acquisition. He asked Ellery Channing to draw a landscape proposal for the woodlot above the pond, intending to create a garden out of the wilderness. Channing's drawing of plantings and curving footpaths brought a little bit of Versailles to the woods, but it slowly occurred to Channing and to Emerson himself that his woodlots would be needed to grow a different kind of plant.

"I want to go soon and live away by the pond where I shall hear only the wind whispering among the reeds. It will be a success if I shall have left myself behind," Thoreau had written in his journal in December of 1841 in the gnomic style that would characterize his later journals. "But my friends ask what I will do when I get there. Will it not be employment enough to watch the progress of the seasons?"

The Thoreau family didn't feel like family anymore, and the Emersons were ready to have their house and their marriage back to themselves. Thoreau had nowhere to go, no other alternative, as Channing reminded him, than to build the shelter that would later inspire William Butler Yeats to write in his homage to Thoreau, "The Lake

Isle of Innisfree," "I will arise and go now." So in early May, Thoreau began preparations to build his hut. He kept careful account of every nail and timber purchase, accounts that constitute the first chapter of the book he would write about his experience, *Walden.*

By this time Thoreau had been poor for a long time. He embraced his want. In fact, he had come to despise the rich, the landowners, and the people who thought they could actually claim the trees and ponds as their property. For him, isolation would not bring *peace come dropping slow.* Thoreau's plan was to write at Walden Pond, specifically to write his book about going north on the river with his brother John, the book that would become *A Week on the Concord and Merrimack Rivers.*

20

WALDEN POND

———◆———

The neighborhood of Walden Pond is only a few miles from the lazy curves of the Concord River, which the Indians had named Musketaquid, meaning "grassy," for its profuse vegetation that floats just below the surface of the clear water. But it feels worlds away. In Thoreau's writing done at Walden Pond, it almost seems as if he is longing for the other landscape and for the landscape of the country of the past.

In true Thoreau fashion, the book about his brother John doesn't mention his brother John; he is referred to as "the other" or as half of "we." There is only one specific reference in an epigraph: "Where'er thou sails't who sailed with me, Though now thou climbest loftier mounts, and fairer rivers does ascend, Be thou my muse, my Brother." Instead, John's beloved memory seems to suffuse the whole trip with an eerie absence. Beginning in a slightly acerbic voice, that voice which would soon become furious in the opening chapters of *Walden*, Thoreau describes the river on which so much life depended.

"The Musketaquid, or Grass-Ground River, though probably as old as the Nile or the Euphrates, did not begin to have a place in civilized history, until the fame of its grassy meadows and its fish attracted settlers out of England in 1635, when it received the other but kindred name of Concord from the first plantation on its banks, which appears to have been commenced in a spirit of peace and harmony. It will be Grass-Ground River as long as grass grows and water runs here; it will be Concord River only while men lead peaceable lives on its banks."

The Hosmer family turned out to help Thoreau raise the frame of his simple house. Then on the Fourth of July, 1845, the twenty-eight-year-old Thoreau packed a few possessions and walked down the Cambridge Turnpike past the Emerson House to Walden Pond, where he began building the walls and windows of his shingle cottage at Wyman's Meadow, set above the summer-blue water. "Yesterday I came here to live," he wrote on July 5 in the opening of a journal that would ultimately, years later, become *Walden*. "My house makes me think of some mountain houses I have seen, which seemed to have a fresher auroral atmosphere about them, as I fancy the halls of Olympus."

The original shack Thoreau built above the pond is gone, sold for scrap and resold, but a replica has been built near the pond on the east side. It sits in a patch of woods at the edge of the parking lot in front of the building that houses the Walden Pond gift shop. Few people go there. On a summer day, my son and I had it to ourselves. It doesn't look like the place where our ideas about man and nature were changed by brilliant thinking and more brilliant writing. It looks like an outbuilding where lumber might be stored, or a gardener's shack. It's a tiny space, hardly as large as the rooms inside a beaver dam or an eagle's nest in a large tree, barely raised off the earth, with just enough room for a narrow bed and a small desk.

Walden Pond is one of many kettle hole ponds in and around Concord, ponds like Flint Pond, Goose Pond, and the pond at the bend in the Sudbury River called Fairhaven Bay where Thoreau took Hawthorne canoeing and later he and Hoar let the fire get out of control. Created by the uneven melting of glacial ice, these ponds are as old as the landscape. Surrounded by thick forests, Walden goes from being a few feet deep to being a hundred feet deep in its less-than-two-mile length. It would become Thoreau's home for two years. Although no one in Concord realized it, and although few would realize it for decades, the shimmering surface of the kettle pond named Walden would be the mirror of Thoreau's genius for generations to come.

Walden would be his raven, his Old Manse, his Margaret Fuller. He had seemingly lost everything—his beloved brother, the only woman he ever loved, the prospect of a literary career, and the prospect of a teaching career. Now his work could begin. In his early days at Walden, he wrote part of a sentence that has now become famous. As an example of the intense and brilliant rewriting that Thoreau put into *Walden* and with which he transformed his raw journals to a great masterpiece, this sentence is hard to beat. "I went to the woods to live deliberately," he wrote, "so that I might front the essential facts of things, and might not, when I came to die, discover that I had not lived."

For years, Thoreau was thought of as an obscure appendage to the great Emerson and the genius Hawthorne. In the eyes of posterity, he seemed to survive only in the shadow of his great neighbors in the same way the women, Louisa May Alcott and Margaret Fuller, had. As he became more and more known in this country in the 1960s and as many of his theories about the relationship of man and nature gained acceptance, he became famous a century after his death. With that well-deserved fame, which is still growing, the question of his sexual orientation was raised. Was Thoreau gay? There is lots of conflicting evidence, including his love for and proposal to Ellen Sewall. On his death bed, he confided to his sister that he had never stopped loving Ellen. He was also entangled with the much younger Louisa May Alcott, and a number of Concord women hoped to become involved with him. One, the Emersons' tutor, Sophia Foord, actually proposed, to his horror.

Some writers, such as Walter Harding in an essay titled "Thoreau's Sexuality" in the *Journal of Homosexuality,* have speculated that he was homosexual, but unlike Emerson and Hawthorne, both men with acknowledged and sometimes troublesome sexual needs, it isn't clear that Thoreau's sexuality affected his life at all. It's a twenty-first-century question directed at an emphatically nineteenth-century per-sonality. What is to be said about a man whose connections to birds and fish and all living things sustained him in a way that his connections to other people could never do?

The Emerson House on the Cambridge Turnpike, called the Concord and Union Turnpike when Emerson bought it from the Coolidge family in 1835 and settled there with his second wife, Lydia Jackson. Built in 1828, the house was called the Coolidge Castle. The Emersons renamed it "Bush."

Dovecote Cottage, owned by the Hosmer family, was the Alcotts' first home in Concord in 1840.

Ellen Tucker of Concord, New Hampshire, Emerson's beloved first wife, who died at the age of twenty of tuberculosis, leaving the money which would support Emerson as well as Thoreau, the Alcotts, and the Hawthornes.

3

Ralph Waldo Emerson, whose encouragement and money created the Concord literary community. "I often say of Emerson that the personality of the man—the wonderful heart and soul of the man, present in all he writes, thinks, does, hopes—goes far toward justifying the whole literary business," Walt Whitman wrote.

4

5

Henry David Thoreau ten years after the publication of *Walden*.

6

The Emerson family in front of their house on the Cambridge Turnpike. Ralph Waldo and Lidian are on either side of the knocker.

A young Louisa May Alcott.   7

8

Alcott in her bedroom at Orchard House, the room where she wrote *Little Women*.

Bronson Alcott on the bench he built in front of Orchard House under the elm. He waited with a pile of apples to give travelers who were then obliged to listen to a philosophical discourse on teaching or the nature of man. Hawthorne, who lived next door, soon refused to come out of the house.

9

Orchard House in the 1860s.

Susan Cheever in front of Orchard House in 2003.

12

Louisa May Alcott after her success.

Brady photo of Hawthorne.

13

Portrait of Nathaniel Hawthorne
by Charles Osgood, 1840.　　14

Margaret Fuller.

15

Photograph of Herman Melville by
Rodney Dewey.   16

21

MARGARET FULLER,
THE SEXY MUSE

———◆———

"In looking for the causes of the great influence possessed by Margaret Fuller over her pupils, companions and friends, I find something in the fact of her unusual truth-speaking power," wrote a friend, Sarah Clarke, after Fuller's death. "She not only did not speak lies after our foolish social customs, but she met you fairly. She broke her lance upon your shield. Encountering her glance, something like an electric shock was felt. Her eye pierced through your disguises. Your outworks fell before her first assault and you were at her mercy."

Many men became entangled with Fuller's combination of erotic power and sexual confusion, but few more than Hawthorne and Emerson. Fuller and Emerson met in 1836, and by 1840 they were working closely on the first issues of *The Dial* and Margaret was spending weeks at a time in the guest room of the Emerson House in Concord. Fuller was unafraid, unafraid of her own brilliance and not afraid to be bitchy. She called Alcott "Plato Skimpole." Hawthorne and Fuller had met in Boston during the exuberant years after he left the little room in the house in Salem where he had spent more than a decade writing stories on a plain pine table reflected in a mahogany-framed mirror—writing in such a fever that his sisters sometimes left his meals outside his door.

Although Hawthorne was secretly engaged to Sophia Peabody, his ambivalence about marriage in general, and about marriage to the slim, obedient, and easily swayed semi-invalid who worshiped him in particular, is clear in his actions. First, he joined the community of Brook Farm, which was often visited by Fuller and Emerson. During the three years of his secret engagement to Peabody and the two years after their marriage, Hawthorne continued to pursue Fuller in his imagination and, as a friend, in life. Hawthorne arrived at Brook Farm during an April snowstorm, and the snowstorm in which he arrives in his novel about his experience, *The Blithedale Romance,* is warmed by the presence of an electrifying, truth-speaking female presence. "Zenobia's aspect . . . impressed itself on me so distinctly, that I can now summon her up like a ghost," he wrote in a description suffused with longing. "She was dressed as simply as possible. . . . but with a silken kerchief between which and her gown there was one glimpse of white shoulder. It struck me as a great piece of good fortune that there should be just that glimpse. Her hair—which was dark, glossy and of singular abundance—was put up rather soberly and primly without curls or other ornament except a single flower. It was an exotic of rare beauty. And as fresh as if the hothouse gardener had just clipt it from the stem. That flower has struck deep root in my memory."

Hawthorne was a rat with women. His combination of handsomeness, tender good manners, and tremendous distance was profoundly attractive, although he had no money and little prospect of making any. Even as he kept Elizabeth Peabody at bay while courting Sophia, he kept Sophia at bay both before and after their marriage while engaging in an intense friendship with Fuller, played out over many summer afternoons lounging on the grass, evenings playing with Una, the Hawthornes' little daughter, boat trips on the lazy summer river, and walks through the Concord woods. When Fuller was away, Emerson dropped in on Hawthorne and talked about her. "He apotheosized her as the greatest woman, I believe, of ancient or modern times," jibed Hawthorne in his journal, "and the one figure in the world worth considering."

Sometimes staying with the Emersons, sometimes staying with the Hawthornes in the Old Manse, sometimes house-sitting for the Channings, Fuller brought an imaginative ferment and light into the lives of the Emerson and Hawthorne families. Lidian Emerson was not pleased. At the Emerson dinner table, she burst into bitter tears to keep Fuller and her husband from taking a walk they had planned. While Fuller and Emerson wrote each other love notes that were carried from room to room, Lidian retired upstairs and rarely came down. Sophia Peabody, on the other hand, took the opposite tack—she claimed to love Fuller more than her husband did.

On a typical afternoon, Margaret ambled down to the edge of the river to wait. There she would sit and read, watch the plants swayed by the current under the glassy surface of the water, or laugh at the ducks that swam and dived around the crumbling abutments of the Old North Bridge beyond where Hawthorne's boat was tied to a tree at the river's edge. "Hawthorne came down about six," she wrote in the ecstatic journal of one evening during those summers, "and we went out on the river and staid till after sunset. We talked a great deal this time. I love him much, & love to be with him in this sweet tender homely scene. But I should like too, to be with him on the bold ocean shore. When we came back Una was lying on the sofa all undrest. She acted like a little wild thing towards me, leaning towards me, stretching out her arms whenever I turned." What was going on in the Hawthornes' marriage? Sophia ostensibly worshiped her husband, and their son Julian, in writing about his parents after their deaths, held their marriage up as sheer perfection. Others, like Thomas Higginson, thought it nothing more than the convenient arrangement of two complete narcissists. Whatever it was, it didn't seem to get in Margaret Fuller's way.

At the Emersons', things were cooler than at the Old Manse. There, feelings were becoming as complicated as the wandering woodland paths along the river where Hawthorne and Fuller meandered at will. "Waldo was here three times yesterday, and sang his song of nature," Fuller writes. "On his lips is the perfumed honey of Hymettus, but we can only sip." During Fuller's earlier visits, she and Emerson had become so close that he, frightened, backed away from her. "I plunge with eagerness into this pleasant element of affection with its haps and harms," he had written her when they were publishing *The Dial* together in 1839. But by 1840, Emerson had cooled, although he reassured Fuller that he would never "go back to his arctic habits."

"Was I not raised out of the society of mere mortals by being chosen the friend of the holiest nun & began instantly to dream of pure confidences & prayers of preserved maids in bodies delicate when a flash of lightning shivers my castle in the air . . ." wrote Emerson. "The fragment of confidence that a wife can give to an old friend is not worth picking up after this invitation to Elysian tables."

Again staying at the Emersons', where Lidian tried to be hospitable although she certainly let it be known that she wasn't happy to be her husband's discarded fragment of confidence, Fuller walked over to the Hawthornes' to bring some potatoes from the Emerson garden and a new rattle for Una. "Hawthorne walked home with me beneath the lovely trembling . . ." A line of X's follows this in the journal. Again and again, Fuller's journals reflect the sting of Emerson's ambivalence and the deliciousness of Hawthorne's friendship.

The warmth of the summer nights, the long afternoon walks, the boat trips they took together, had a huge effect on both Fuller and Hawthorne. They seemed struck by the midsummer night's dream, the madness that envelops lovers on hot summer nights. Somehow, now that he was married, Hawthorne seemed more able to give himself over to Fuller than had been possible with other women in the past. Forming her feminist views, Fuller was outspokenly aware of the way marriage was a trap for the women she knew. At the same time, she was often sharply aware of what she was missing. "With the intellect I always have always shall overcome," she wrote later in 1844, "but that is not half of the work. The life, the life Oh my God! Shall the life never be sweet?"

22

ROME

———◆———

Standing in the Emerson House guest room where Fuller stayed when she was at the Emersons', it's hard not to notice that Emerson's study is a few feet away across the hall, while the rest of the Emerson family is safely tucked away upstairs. What really went on in that small double bed with its white chenille spread across from the windows looking out over Emerson's lawns? What really happened when Fuller and Hawthorne, long after midnight, laughed their way up from a long talk seated on the moss next to the river near the buttresses of the Old North Bridge? Was there kissing? Was there sex? Both Emerson and Hawthorne had their sexual sides, as their large families attest. Lidian's angry response to Emerson's long friendship with Fuller, and Fuller's apologies to Emerson for the trouble she has caused in their marriage certainly sound like the destructive side of infidelity.

But the middle of the nineteenth century was a time when sexual energy was pent up in this country, and all these people were high-minded prudes, usually too wrapped up in Goethe to be thinking about the carnal aspect of love. Even Walt Whitman had joined the popular antimasturbation movement. None of them drank. Perhaps the absence of actual physical intercourse, with its groping with the endless skirts of the time, made the affairs of Emerson and Hawthorne with Fuller even more intense than they might have been otherwise. The only thing more powerful than lust is lust denied.

After she left Concord, Fuller had a series of unhappy love affairs, and finally in Rome she met Count Giovanni Ossoli. But the Margaret

Fuller who reported on the Roman Revolution of 1848–49 and ran a hospital there was a different woman than the brilliant, sunny woman who spent her time in Concord deep in conversation with both Emerson and Hawthorne. The conversations may have been physically innocent, but in the end they were more powerful for being connections of the heart rather than the body.

Emerson, for all his friendship with both Fuller and Hawthorne, was not pleased by what he saw developing between them. Emerson supported both Fuller, through *The Dial,* and Hawthorne, by securing him a home at the Old Manse, even though months went by when Hawthorne was unable to pay the rent. Emerson was a complicated character, a sorrowing man of many losses, a brilliant intellect who could distill experience into startling essays, an unhappy husband, a great lecturer and teacher. In the spirit of generosity and companionship, he had brought all his friends to Concord: the Alcotts, the Hawthornes, and Fuller. He was also often supporting Thoreau. Sometimes he just seemed to get sick of the whole thing, of paying for everyone, of being the oldest and most careful of them, of being the one who had to act like an adult.

Something snapped that day when he came on Margaret and Hawthorne laughing as they lay on the grass, and by September the Hawthornes had heard from the Reverend Samuel Ripley that he wanted his house back, thank you very much. He and his wife Sarah had decided to move from Waltham back to Concord. "We were actually turned out of roof and home," Sophia wailed to Hawthorne's sister Louisa. The Old Manse had been their home when they were newlyweds. It had been so much their home that Sophia and her husband had spent a long time one April evening passing Sophia's diamond ring back and forth in an inspired act of vandalism, scratching their thoughts in the window pane of Hawthorne's study on the second floor. Standing there now as evening falls, time stops. It feels as if your hosts have just gone downstairs to dinner, leaving you this portrait of their marriage written in diamond on glass.

Man's accidents are God's purposes Sophia A. Hawthorne 1843
Nath Hawthorne This is his study
The smallest twig leans clear against the sky

Composed by my wife and written with her diamond
Inscribed by my husband at sunset, April 3 1843. In the Gold light.
SAH

It was their house, and at that moment it felt as if they would be there forever.

Now the Hawthornes had nowhere to go, but they were told they could stay until November. Immediately, though, a team of carpenters appeared to renovate the house for the new tenants. They tore down the woodbine that grew up one side of the house, and covered the lawn with wood chips, and shattered the silence with their hammers and saws. "We gathered up our household goods, drank a farewell cup of tea in our pleasant little breakfast room . . . and passed forth between the tall stone gate posts as uncertain as the wandering Arabs where our tent might next be pitched," Hawthorne wrote.

Their old rooms in the Herbert Street house in Salem had been rented, so Hawthorne moved into the upstairs bedroom and his wife and children rented a room at the bottom of the house. "Here I am again established in the old chamber where I wasted so many years of my life," the humiliated Hawthorne wrote to his friend Bridge. As always, when things went badly for Hawthorne, he took up his pen and began to write.

In 1846, Margaret Fuller became the first woman editor of Horace Greeley's *Tribune* in New York City. That same year, through a great deal of influence being brought to bear by his Democratic friends Horatio Bridge, Franklin Pierce, and others, on April 3, 1846, Hawthorne secured a job as the surveyor of the Salem Custom House and was finally able to provide a steady income for his wife and two children— his son, Julian, was also born in June of 1846. He stopped writing. In August, after a farewell visit from Emerson, who came to Cambridgeport to say goodbye, Fuller left for England and Italy as the first woman foreign correspondent for Greeley.

As a customs inspector, Hawthorne found the work of examining what came in and out of the sleepy port of Salem pleasant and not too taxing. The salary of $1,200 a year was just enough to support the family and to gradually pay off his old Concord debts—one to the Reverend Samuel Ripley for back rent. As the secretary of the Salem

Lyceum, Hawthorne brought Emerson and Thoreau to lecture.

Always an object of scandal, Fuller's involvement with the Roman Revolution and her connection to Count Giovanni Ossoli had all of Concord buzzing in her absence. News traveled from Concord to Salem and back through visits and letters. Fuller hadn't bothered to get married, they said. Ossoli was a Catholic whose family had disinherited him; Ossoli was not much more than a servant; Ossoli came from a great Roman family, and if she had married him, Margaret would be a Marquesa. Then in 1848 came the news that Margaret was pregnant with an illegitimate child. Then the news was that Margaret had given birth to an illegitimate child. Fuller and Ossoli took an apartment in Florence on the Piazza Santa Maria Novella and joined the large American and English expatriate community.

"The American authoress, Miss Fuller . . . has taken us by surprise in Florence," wrote her new friend Elizabeth Barrett Browning, "retiring from the Roman field with a husband and a child above a year old. Nobody had even suspected a word of this underplot, and her American friends stood in mute astonishment before this apparition of them here. The husband is a Roman marquis, appearing amiable and gentlemanly, and having fought well, they say, at the siege, but with no pretension to cope with his wife on any ground appertaining to the intellect."

Hawthorne heard the news of Margaret from Sophia, from his sisters, from everyone. Was it true she had become good friends with Robert Browning and Elizabeth Barrett Browning? What would happen when Margaret came home with her illegitimate son and her lover, an Italian? Perhaps Margaret had married this Count Ossoli. William Ellery Channing was telling everyone that was impossible, that Margaret was too much of a free thinker to submit to the institution of marriage. Emerson disagreed. "When it came to be a practical question to herself," he wrote in an unpublished note to himself, "she would have felt that this was a tie which deserved every solemn sanction, that against the other was a vast public opinion too vast to brave."

23

THE MARGARET GHOST

———◆———

Then in June 1849, Hawthorne was abruptly removed from the job that had provided the first financial stability in his life. The Whig victory of the new President Zachary Taylor meant that all Democratic appointments were in danger. Hawthorne, outraged, wrote a letter protesting his dismissal in the *Boston Daily Advertiser.* A prominent Salem Whig, Charles Upham, attacked him in the Salem paper. The Democrats counter-attacked, saying that Hawthorne's appointment had been an honor extended to him as a writer. The Whigs hauled out a record of Hawthorne's political activities, including his attendance at torchlight parades. "The dismissal of Mr. Surveyor Hawthorne became a cause célèbre throughout New England," Hawthorne biographer Randall Stewart writes. This was not the kind of fame Hawthorne had dreamed of. He was becoming notorious, and no one even knew that he had written *Mosses from an Old Manse* and *Twice-Told Tales.* Now, to make it worse, he hadn't written much more than a few pages in almost five years.

In the meantime, his mother was getting sicker by the day. "I love my mother," Hawthorne wrote after one of his last visits to her, "but there has been ever since my boyhood, a sort of coldness of intercourse between us, such as is apt to come between people of strong feelings. . . . I was moved to kneel down close to my mother, and take her hand." Kneeling at the bedside, listening to his mother's murmured wishes that he take care of his sisters, Hawthorne broke down. It was all too much. He shook with sobs. Later he wrote, "Surely it is the darkest hour I ever lived."

It was Henry James who dubbed Fuller "the Margaret Ghost," and it was Hawthorne who seems to have been most haunted by her. After his mother's death in July, the unemployed Hawthorne was so desperate, so manic, so driven by despair that he was afflicted with what he called a "brain fever." Then one day he went upstairs to his study and began a book about a courageous, beautiful woman with an illegitimate child, a woman who believed in women's rights and preferred to live alone rather than compromise her integrity. He poured out his longing with the fire of a writer who has not written in years and wrote his finest novel, one that would catapult him to the right kind of fame and make his literary ambitions come true. "He writes immensely," Sophia reported to her mother as her husband worked nine hours a day, day after day, on his book.

By February of 1850, the book was finished, and so moving that when Hawthorne read Sophia the last chapter it sent her to bed with a headache. Margaret was still alive, if abroad, and it's no wonder that her husband's thinly veiled admiration caused a migraine. Hawthorne's publisher, James Fields, loved the book and published it on March 15 to great literary acclaim and some satisfying moral outrage. It immediately became a best-seller.

24

HAWTHORNE LEAVES
SALEM FOREVER

◆

Nathaniel Hawthorne's reputation in Salem after the publication of *The Scarlet Letter,* the real beginning of his career as a significant writer, got much worse. After the political accusations and counter-accusations surrounding his dismissal from the Custom House, his nonfiction account of *The Custom-House*, published as the introduction to *The Scarlet Letter* set off another firestorm of gossip and criticism.

In the story in which Hawthorne frames his tale of betrayal and adultery, he is working in the Salem Custom House, a sleepy, lazy sort of place, when he happens upon the manuscript telling the history of the scarlet *A*. "It contributes greatly towards a man's moral and intellectual health," he wrote with unconscious arrogance, "to be brought into habits of companionship with individuals unlike himself, who care little for his pursuits." His portrait of his coworkers, which, he wrote to his friend Horatio Bridge, he thought had been good-natured, did not seem at all good-natured to them. The local paper reflected the town's outrage at "small sneers at Salem, and by vilifying some of his former associates." In other words, Hawthorne had come to the point where he needed to get out of Dodge. "If I escape town without being tarred and feathered," he wrote Bridge, "I shall consider it good luck."

It wasn't just the relatively bland description of the local businessmen that offended people. In his description of a tangle of human failings set in the seventeenth century before the Salem Witch Trials, he had dropped the equivalent of a moral hand grenade. Readers of *The Scarlet Letter* are forced to examine the ways in which people are fooled into betraying each other, and the way in which fear can make neighbors into lethal weapons. They were forced to examine the institution of marriage and its connection to child-bearing. The people of Salem had had quite enough of examining such things.

But Hawthorne was not sorry. Like his heroine who had taken the plain fabric *A* inflicted on her as punishment and made it beautiful by embroidering it with gold "with so much fertility and gorgeous luxuriance of fancy" so that it "transfigured the wearer," Hawthorne had taken the sins that the proper men and women of Salem and Concord abhorred—adultery, the birth of an illegitimate child, sexual secrecy—and made them sympathetic. He had made the redoubtable Hester Prynne a single mother for the ages, a woman both lovable and resilient. The goodwives of Salem would not quickly forgive him.

Before, Hawthorne had been a writer of tales. He had the prestige of being a writer, but his work hadn't really been read by the general populace. In *The Scarlet Letter,* Hawthorne's talents blossomed into a novel that is still powerful, and to his amazement people seemed to take it personally. But readers do take novels personally. He and his family were no longer welcome in Salem, the town where he had grown up and spent much of his adult life, and the town of his ancestors. In fact, the heroic Hester showed more fortitude than Hawthorne. After her release from prison, she did not choose to leave Salem, even though she was generally scorned and risked being separated from her child. "Here, she said to herself, had been the scene of her guilt, and here should be the scene of her earthly punishment."

Hawthorne was not interested in earthly punishment. Hester had wanted to stay near the father of her child. Hawthorne's family was at his disposal. Once again the Hawthornes were house-hunting on a limited budget, this time with two children. In choosing to court and marry Sophia Hawthorne rather than her more forceful older sister or the other women he was involved with in Salem, Hawthorne showed a personal shrewdness that helped him until the end of his life. He traded passion for stability, troublesome intellectual companionship for an artistic woman who would never get over being grateful.

Sophia Hawthorne was well accustomed to moves caused by

poverty. She had grown up in a family with a father who was a doctor at a time when medicine had very little understanding of what made the human body sick or what could heal. Dr. Peabody was phenomenally unsuccessful at his chosen profession; he lacked the one thing that doctors could actually provide in the nineteenth century, which was the ability to project some kind of comfort and reassurance. In a variety of schemes to stay afloat, he moved his family of three girls and three boys up to New Hampshire and back again, out to Brookline west of Boston and back again. Out to Salem and back again.

In many cases, we now know, the cures propagated by nineteenth-century doctors were worse than the original disease. Many patients died on the operating table infected by the unwashed hands of their surgeons. One of the worst medications used in the mid nineteenth century was a large dose of calomel or mercury, which was recommended for almost everything—as a guard against typhoid and as a cure for headaches and frayed nerves. In fact, calomel, the nineteenth-century doctor's name for mercury, attacks the human central nervous system and causes irreparable damage. Many women in the 1800s would be overdosed with calomel and have their bodies destroyed from within by the medication that was supposed to heal their nerves.

By the time Nathaniel Hawthorne appeared in her life, Sophia had been dosed with a lot of calomel and was certainly an opium addict— opium being another drug thoughtlessly dispensed to men and women in pain. She suffered from migraine headaches that nothing could help, but the headaches combined with the destructive "cures" applied by her incompetent father had reduced her to what her doctor, Walter Channing, called a "bed case." Bed cases were common in those days of bad medicine combined with the very limited lives offered to women. Their choices often came down to being pathetic spinsters, marrying men they hated who acted as if they were servants and moved them wherever they liked, or staying in bed being waited on and worried over by their families for the rest of their lives.

With her younger-sister shrewdness, considering the choices she had, Sophia had chosen to be a bed case. During one year, she imagined she was close to death. Only a passionate interest in a much older new doctor—the brilliant Channing—had changed that. Channing prescribed activity, travel, and the pursuit of the painting and drawing career that gave Sophia so much pleasure. As a result, she spent time in Cuba and launched herself as an artist. After Channing married another woman—someone with an income and closer to his own age—Sophia found herself spending more and more time in bed.

Enter Nathaniel Hawthorne. No matter what Hawthorne did, his moods, his sulks, his three years of dithering during their secret engagement, his infatuations with other women, nothing could shake the huge improvement in Sophia's life which being his wife entailed. She was still quite sick—mercury poisoning is irreversible—and she still turned to opium for her headaches, but Hawthorne had given her a life and she never forgot that. Now, moving because her husband had no money, even with two small children, was small stuff for the woman who had already been to hell and back at the hands of her own family.

25

STOCKBRIDGE

———◆———

In September, Sophia left Salem to visit her friend Caroline Sturgis Tappan, who, with her wealthy husband, William Aspinall Tappan, had leased an estate called Highwood in the Berkshires. The estate included a small red farmhouse, a warren of small rooms crammed into one and a half stories, with lovely views of the valley and surrounding mountains. The Tappans were eager to have the Hawthornes as neighbors—they imagined themselves assembling an Emersonian community farther west—and they offered the house rent-free. As Sophia had known, something always appeared if you were patient. But the idea of living rent-free was too much for the proud and prescient Hawthornes, who insisted on paying $75 for a four-year lease. It seemed like a great bargain.

By June, the Hawthorne family was settled in the little house, where Sophia hung red curtains in the windows and put the familiar family pictures of Correggio's *Madonna* and Raphael's *Transfiguration* on the walls. She placed on the center table the punch bowl that Hawthorne's father had had made in India and created an upstairs study for Hawthorne. "I find it very agreeable to get rid of politics and the rest of that damnable turmoil that has disturbed me for three or four years past," Hawthorne wrote.

The winter and two summers which the Hawthornes spent in the little red house on the Tappan estate and through the generosity of the Tappans, were a sort of Babylonian captivity from the towns—Salem and Concord—that were their true homes. Like the man in the Arab story who meets Death in the market in Damascus and is terrified by the look of surprise on the face of the Grim Reaper, Hawthorne seemed to be avoiding his fate, a fate that eventually caught up with him in the form of the Alcotts, Emerson, and the little town on the winding Concord River. When the man in the Arab story flees to Samarra, Death meets him there, of course. And in a final explanation, Death says that's why he was surprised to see his victim in Damascus when, after all, they had an appointment in Samarra.

Hawthorne may have left political turmoil behind, but he took his restless heart with him everywhere. He had become a family man, a father who adored his children and loved to play with them and write about them. He was a man who was somehow released into a new kind of love in the safety of his own home, as his lovely book, *Twenty Days with Julian and Little Bunny,* about being alone with Julian, reveals. With his children, Hawthorne became an adventurer, a great tree climber and kite flyer and swimmer. At home he became wild, almost as if compensating for his public tameness. In another way, Hawthorne was always carrying on outside the home as well. He was a man of secret lives, of doubleness, whose understanding of deceit and betrayal perfumes his greatest scenes.

At the end of July came the dreadful news that Margaret Fuller had been drowned in a shipwreck. There was an emptiness in Hawthorne's heart that needed filling. On August 5, the Hawthornes went to a picnic and a climb up the local Monument Mountain with their Stockbridge neighbor Dudley Field, Oliver Wendell Holmes, who was vacationing in the Berkshires, and Herman Melville—a writer famous for his shipboard dramas—who was staying in nearby Pittsfield, Massachusetts, at a farm owned by his cousin.

26

MELVILLE

———◆———

The day of the August picnic, in which the group merrily ranged from being caught in the rain to climbing over the ledges to visiting an ice glen, a cold cave in the mountains, has become a landmark in American literary history. The first account of the intense playfulness between Holmes, Melville, and Hawthorne that day appeared almost immediately in a magazine called *Literary World.* It was Sophia who was particularly enchanted by the bushy-bearded writer Herman Melville, whose novels, *Typee, Omoo, Redburn,* and *White-Jacket,* based on his experience as a sailor in the South Seas, Tahiti, and Eimeo, had sold well and given him an extensive reputation as the man who had lived among cannibals. Melville, tanned, lithe, and fourteen years younger, had led the kind of life Hawthorne could only dream about: signing on to the whaler *Acushnet* and then jumping ship, battling great storms and dropping anchor in peaceful faraway lagoons, living with exotic natives who wore flowers instead of clothes. Melville complemented Hawthorne's reserve with an exuberance and tolerance that seemed strange and wonderful to the man forever pacing in the trap of his ancestors' own greed and Puritanism. Hawthorne invited Melville to come and visit at the red house.

Much has been written about the brief, intense, erotic, platonic, literary friendship between Hawthorne and Melville that played itself out during the time the Hawthornes lived in the Berkshires. Melville, a successful writer of books that combined adventure with travel, based on his own firsthand experience, had already embarked on a book about whaling that was to be based on his time on the *Acushnet* and on other whalers' accounts, especially the reports of the sinking of the ship *Essex* by a vengeful white whale. Even as Melville's fearless emotional playfulness seemed to inspire Hawthorne, the older man's high seriousness shifted the course of Melville's book. "Already I feel that this Hawthorne has dropped germinous seeds into my soul," Melville wrote ecstatically in a review of *Mosses from an Old Manse.* "He expands and deepens down the more I contemplate him and further and further shoots his strong New England roots into the hot soil of my southern soul."

In his upstairs study, Hawthorne was working on *The House of the Seven Gables,* a novel about the curse of Salem and the way an ugly past can contaminate even an innocent present. Melville's influence may have made him more prone to the novel's unlikely happy ending. But his influence on Melville is unmistakable. *Moby-Dick* is not like any other work of Melville's, or like any other novel written in that century or any other century. Hawthorne's intensity, his refusal to treat life as anything less than a controlling metaphor for man's moral nature, seemed to be contagious. Armed with wonderful details culled from his own experience, Melville embraced the idea of seriousness, of a literature that could be a moral guide as well as an entertainment. With typical exuberance, he wrote a novel whose first third is devoted to a tender, astonishing homoerotic friendship between the narrator, Ishmael, and his reserved, exotic, highly moral friend Queequeg. The fact that Queequeg is no Yankee but rather an islander hardly disguises the passionate feelings Melville poured into the friendship that redeems the bleakness of his book. He dedicated the book to his friend Nathaniel Hawthorne.

Although both men had lost their fathers in childhood, Hawthorne's loss had sent him back upstairs to bed for twelve years, while Melville turned outward to the world beyond New England. Hawthorne had never been to Europe, and when he finally would get there, it would be in the safest possible way—as an appointee of his friend the president of the United States. Melville had already been around the world, fallen in and out of love with islands and their inhabitants, weathered moral and climatic storms that were somewhere beyond even Hawthorne's imagination. And it was Melville who hailed Hawthorne as a writer of Shakespeare's stature, a man who made Washington Irving look like a grasshopper, the man whose books would become the great American classics.

Was Melville enchanted by Hawthorne's reserve? Or did he indulge his own untamed desires in Hawthorne's direction because he knew there was no chance of Hawthorne returning his passionate regard? Although Hawthorne wrote again and again about the way in which the passionate dashed their lives against the bulwark of the more reserved, he didn't seem to see that his friendship with Melville was doomed. "Hawthorne was a fastidious man who depended on regulation— regular living, regular loving, rituals of predictable routine," writes his biographer Brenda Wineapple, "as if to contain or curb his sense of the underside of things, that stuff of terror and despair and dissolution."

Certainly, Melville was Pan to Hawthorne's Apollo, the suitor rather than the pursued, and the effect of the friendship on his work was both miraculous and disastrous. The seriousness and allegorical use of adventures on the high seas that make *Moby-Dick* such a sustaining novel, one that rewards endless study, did nothing more than annoy Melville's regular readership. The completion of Melville's greatest book, the vast moral novel, the mysterious world he had been able to spin out of his glad imagination while inspired by his taciturn friend, also signaled the end of Melville's career. When the two met, he had been a successful young writer. When they parted, Melville was desperate, unable to support his wife and children, and ultimately resigned to another one of those custom-house jobs that he hated with every fiber of his being.

There are many theories about the destructive power of Hawthorne's friendship on Melville, although none of them go so far as to compare it with the destructive power of Hawthorne's friendship on the unfortunate Margaret Fuller. The literary critic Lewis Mumford accused Hawthorne of ruining Melville by using him as a template for the morally bankrupt main character of his story "Ethan Brand." Since "Ethan Brand" was written before the two men met, this is impossible, but the suspicion remains.

In 1850, Melville was on top of the world, the most generous of men, able to love men and women, a man who had experienced all kinds of things and couldn't wait to experience more. Hawthorne had never yet been on a ship. He had hardly left New England. The closest he came to real travel was watching the great schooners tack in and out of Salem Harbor and up to the docks where he worked as a customs officer. He loved the sea, but from a safe distance. In the years after the publication of *Moby-Dick,* Hawthorne made a few attempts to help his friend, but nothing worked.

Five years later, when Melville visited Hawthorne in Liverpool where Hawthorne had accepted a questionable appointment from his friend President Franklin Pierce, he was a saddened man in need of an income. Their situations were reversed. Melville had been sick, suffering from what Hawthorne called "neuralgic complaints in his head and limbs." The day he visited, it was raining as it always seemed to be raining in Liverpool. He was on his way to the Holy Land in search of something unnamed and perhaps unattainable.

Melville brought along a manuscript—as failing writers often do when they visit their successful friends. He hoped that Hawthorne might help him get the novel, titled *The Confidence-Man,* published. Melville looked, Hawthorne wrote in his notebook, "much the same as he used to do (a little paler, and perhaps a little sadder) in a rough outside coat. . . . I felt rather awkward at first; because this is the first time I have met him since my ineffectual attempt to get him a consular appointment from General Pierce."

Hawthorne had reached the end of his ability or his willingness to help his friend. Instead, the two spent a few pleasant days together drinking and smoking cigars. They visited the nearby town of Chester, where they ate veal pies, toured the cathedral, and drank stout at the Yacht Inn. They were shown the window where Jonathan Swift had written an attack on the clergy, scratched into the glass with a diamond ring. When they got back to Liverpool, Melville left his trunk with the Hawthornes and promised to come back for it. The two men who had spent so many nights in a fury of conversation that seemed as important as life and death no longer had much to say to each other.

27

THE RAILROAD

———◆———

The poet Henry Wadsworth Longfellow often dropped by the Emerson House from his house in nearby Sudbury for a cigar and some brandy, and Emerson, Longfellow, and Hawthorne and his friend Melville talked a lot about who would write the story of Evangeline—they decided that Longfellow was the one. Emerson's influence spread wider than his purse strings—Walt Whitman was a fan who said that Emerson had lit him on fire; Poe revered him.

Not only did he assemble them in Concord, he then invited the Alcotts, Hawthorne, Fuller, Thoreau, and other friends to participate in something called the Transcendental Club, a loose-knit group of men and one woman who got together to discuss important things whenever the Reverend Frederic Hedge, a friend of Emerson's from Maine, came to town. "Who knows but the wise men in an hour more timid or more gracious may crave the aid of wise & blessed women at their session?" he asked. Always the master of indirection and elusiveness, Emerson in his letters can almost always be interpreted two or three ways. Margaret Fuller took the meaning that suited her.

Emerson was always a combination of passionate and rational, of heart and head—an enthusiastic friend and a keeper of account books down to the last penny. His ledgers show that he was the family banker, and that each dollar of income and expense was carefully tracked in the Emerson House. Nowhere is this ambivalence clearer than in Emerson's dealing with the Fitchburg Railroad, which began in June of 1844 running four trains a day from Boston to Concord and on to Fitchburg and back. Henry Adams remarked in his masterful *The Education of Henry Adams* that eighteenth-century Boston came to an end with the first trains of the Boston & Albany Railroad.

In a sleepy backwater like Concord, the impact of the railroad was even more extreme. Massachusetts was to grow 34.8 percent during the 1840s, and Concord water traffic had already been affected by the completion of the Boston-to-Lowell line in 1836. The Fitchburg Railroad began buying land in 1842, and the rails, built along an 18-foot-high earth embankment, had reached Waltham by the time Thoreau went off to Staten Island to teach young William Emerson. The new railroad line passed so close to the west end of Walden Pond on its way through Wyman Meadow to the railroad depot that the pond had to be filled in and built up for the embankment that held the rails. The berm was visible from almost every point in the pond.

The woods around the Emerson House were filled with the hundreds of Irish workers and their families who had come to complete the huge construction project. "The town is full of Irish and the woods of engineers with theodolite and red flag singing out their feet and inches to each other from station to station," Emerson complained in a letter to the absent Thoreau. "I hope you will not be washed away by the Irish Sea," Thoreau wrote to his sister.

Emerson joined Hawthorne in lamenting the end of the old ways brought by the new railroad, its arrival celebrated by a gala opening on Bunker Hill Day in 1844. He thought of moving. When he heard the train's whistle, he wrote in his journal, "Wherever that music comes, it has a sequel. . . . Whew! Whew! Whew! How is real estate here in the swamp and wilderness? Whew! Whew! down with that forest on the side of the hill. I want ten thousand chestnut sleepers." He moaned that the railroad had reduced men to chattel, "who could be transported by the box and the ton." This was Emerson the poet. Emerson the accountant buckled down and sold a slice of his Walden Pond woodlot to the Fitchburg Railroad for their tracks. Later he invested in railroad stock.

Thoreau objected as well. "The iron horse makes the hills echo with his snort like thunder, shaking the earth with his feet, and breathing fire and smoke from his nostrils." Nevertheless, he was also able to make a practical use of the coming of the railroad. When the company auctioned off the shanties that had been used to house their workers, Thoreau bought some of them for materials to build a shed in back of the Thoreau house out of which the family ran the pencil business. Later, another worker's shanty, bought for $4.25 from James Collins, was dismantled, had its nails drawn and its wood dried out in the sun to be adapted to the frame for Thoreau's house on Walden Pond.

28

COMMUNITY

———◆———

In 1845, as Emerson's friend Thoreau began planning his cabin at Walden, Edgar Allan Poe published "The Raven." Margaret Fuller was living in New York, falling in love with a man named James Nathan, and working for Horace Greeley. The Hawthornes had moved back to Salem, and Emerson started a new series of lectures about Great Men. In the years to come after the Tucker money had been spent, lecturing would be Emerson's bread and butter—he sometimes gave eighty lectures a year, traveling all over New England and to Ohio. Tall and loose-jointed, with a head carried ahead of his narrow shoulders, a beaky nose, and piercing blue eyes, Emerson would give a lecture, spend the night, and take a train to his next destination for the next night's lecture. His subjects ranged from Great Men to German Literature to "The Conduct of Life" and he was often away from Concord for weeks and months at a time. Who can blame him?

Lidian, once his slender, independent helpmeet, had retired to the upper rooms of the house, overwhelmed by the work of her own family and still grieving over the loss of her son. Her worst moments, copied down by Emerson in his journal and then scratched out, are easy to imagine from her words: "Dear husband, I wish I had never been born. I do not see how God can compensate me for the sorrow of existence." Later, Emerson called her "my poor broken wife."

Emerson was not admired by everyone—some thought his lectures absurdly overblown—but there was no shortage of a demand in the system of local lyceums that had grown up across New England. He traveled from Gloucester to Lowell to Worcester to Providence to Boston and back to the North Shore. Drained by what seemed like endless traveling, sleeping in country inn after country inn or the dingy guest rooms of his lecture hosts, by the fall of 1847, Emerson was ready for a change.

29

WITHOUT MARGARET

In October 1847, Emerson boarded the packet *Washington Irving* bound for Liverpool, for an extended stay in England and visits to France. He left Thoreau in charge of things at home in Concord. Did he plan to see Margaret Fuller, who had sailed for England just a year earlier? He had certainly been reading her letters to the *Tribune* describing the British working classes, and he had written the note that served as her introduction to his friend the great Thomas Carlyle. "Carlyle indeed is arrogant and overbearing," she wrote for the *Tribune,* "but in his arrogance there is no littleness or self-love; it is the heroic arrogance of some old Scandinavian conqueror. . . . You do not love him, perhaps, nor revere, and perhaps, also, he would only laugh at you if you did; but you like him heartily, and like to see him the powerful Smith, the Siegfried, melting all the old iron in his furnace till it glows to a sunset red and burns you if you senselessly go too near."

Fuller, absorbing England as a journalist as well as a scholar, had already met Carlyle's friend Giuseppe Mazzini, the exiled leader of the Italian Republican movement. Inspired by Mazzini's ascetic singleness of purpose—he lived on nothing in England while waiting for a chance to return to Italy—Margaret got her first taste of the Italian temper that would change her life. But she was ahead of her old friend by about a year and about a lifetime. The witty single woman he remembered, roaming over the society he knew so well looking for a place she might perch for a moment, was gone.

By the time Emerson landed in Liverpool, Margaret had already gone south to France and then to Italy. In fact, she was living in Rome with Count Giovanni Ossoli, the man who would be the father of her child. In England, Emerson came close to quarreling with Carlyle. Was the presence of Margaret and her sly criticism of the great man somehow hovering between them? Eighteen forty-eight was a year of revolution: in England with the Chartist movement, in France with the overthrow of Louis Philippe, and in the disintegration of Italy.

Being so close to each other, first in England then in Paris where Margaret had gone to see George Sand and hear Chopin play, seemed to bring these old friends closer than ever. When Margaret was across the hall, Emerson knew that he had to keep his distance. One wrong move would have brought down everything he had built for himself. Now that she was across a continent and they were both far from Concord, he began trying to get closer to her.

Distance was their aphrodisiac, and their letters back and forth are warmer and more open than previous letters. Did Emerson also sense that Margaret, who had always somehow belonged to him, had now floated out of his grasp and into another world of motherhood and partnership? When she wrote him glumly about being sick without mentioning that she was sick because she was pregnant, he responded immediately, "Come live with me at Concord."

But when he wrote a letter telling Lidian back in Concord of his proposal that Margaret live with them, Thoreau reported, Lidian turned as yellow as saffron and bombarded her husband with tragic letters asking him to rescind the invitation. His longing to reach out to Margaret seemed to grow more intense as Lidian protested and Margaret found her new life. In March, he invited her to come and meet him in Paris. She declined, saying that her health had been bad. Emerson urged her to leave Italy, which was clearly a place that was bad for her health. "Can you not safely take the first steamer to Marseilles, come to Paris and go home with me," he asked. It was too late.

In the meantime, Emerson's badly timed longing to take care of Margaret was exacerbated by the news from home. His absent family was thriving with Thoreau as the head of the household. Thoreau wrote Emerson that Lidian is "a very dear sister to me." He had banked the apple and pear trees, and one day as he played with Emerson's three-year-old son Eddy, Eddy asked Thoreau, "Will you be my father?" On July 15, Emerson boarded the *Europa* and sailed for home alone; on September 5, aged thirty-eight and attended by a local midwife in the hill town of Rieti, Margaret gave birth to a baby, and she and his father named him Angelino.

On his return home, Emerson had to quell a different kind of revolution than those he had seen and read about in England and France. Thoreau was caring for his children, and Lidian, who had become so dampened by grief, seemed to be cheered by the younger man. Thoreau didn't approve of Emerson's European travels or his nattering on about Germany and Carlyle. Emerson was sick of Thoreau's self-righteous simplicity—a simplicity he had so often had to subsidize with his own hard-earned money.

Thoreau moved out, and Emerson, who was very glad to be home, had his gladness dimmed by his family's obvious longing for his friend. It was hard, after all his generosity, to find that his brand of maturity wasn't as lovable as his disciple's brand of immaturity. When Thoreau's book *A Week on the Concord and Merrimack Rivers* was finally published thanks largely to Emerson's efforts, Emerson apparently stopped biting his tongue. "While my friend was my friend he flattered me and I never heard the truth from him," wrote the wounded Thoreau. "But when he became my enemy he shot it to me on a poisoned arrow."

As he aged and had absolutely no success in his chosen field, as his world crumbled around him and failure became his expectation, Thoreau seemed to become more and more rigid. All he had were his principles. Instead of believing in them, he seemed to be ruled by them. Ask him how his day was going and you'd get some kind of incoherent and slightly patronizing response about the habits of the chipmunk in the winter or the architecture of a beaver dam or the feeding patterns of the spotted owl. As grief and sorrow seemed to make Emerson more responsible, and as it drove him to work harder, the same forces seemed to make Thoreau less responsible. It wasn't a good trend for the two men's friendship. "Henry David Thoreau is like the wood God who solicits the wandering poet and draws him into antres vast and deserts idle and bereaves him of his memory," Emerson wrote with a cruelty stemming from impatience. "And leaves him naked, plaiting vine and with twigs in his hand. Very seductive are the first steps from the town into the woods, but the end is want and madness."

Part Three

30

LOUISA MAY ALCOTT
RETURNS

———◆———

In the winter of 1844, the Alcotts returned to Concord, not for the first or last time. Abigail's father's estate had yielded $1,000 and Emerson contributed $500 so that Abba could buy Hillside, Horatio Cogswell's pig farm on the Lexington Road across and to the west of the Emerson House. Bronson protested; he wanted nothing to do with property or commerce. Throughout their friendship, Bronson was able to claim that he didn't care about property, while Emerson paid for the property he and his family needed.

The house was a mess; it had been an old wreck when the British retreated past it down the Lexington Road in 1775. Since then, few improvements had been made. Cogswell had let his pigs have the run of the place, which had four low-ceilinged rooms and a few falling-down outbuildings. Bronson Alcott was by now a competent gardener and carpenter. He began on the house, dividing the huge downstairs rooms and building a new story, and he planned a series of terraces in the hill behind. The pasture on the other side of the road ran down to a brook, and Bronson planted a stand of trees to shelter the family bathing place from those passing on the road.

The next four years were a relatively peaceful and abundant time for the Alcott family. Compared to the adventure of Fruitlands, almost anything would have seemed secure and comfortable. They took in Sophia Foord as a boarder; she had also boarded with the Emersons.

She tutored the children and took them on long, delicious walks in the woods. To his deep chagrin, Henry David Thoreau had somehow excited Miss Foord's passionate desire. She decided she was in love with him; they were meant for each other. When Thoreau came to visit his friend Bronson, things were quite exciting at Hillside. On other afternoons, the Alcotts, or just Louisa, visited Thoreau in his cabin on Walden Pond.

Once again, Louisa fell in love with the boyish man who seemed to be at one with nature. He showed her how the bluebird carried the sky on its back and how the scarlet tanager looked to be about to set fire to the leaves. Out on the pond, lazily drifting in Thoreau's boat, he played the flute, and Louisa felt that the water had become part of the same element as the sky and that she and her childhood teacher had floated into another dimension.

Louisa May Alcott turned fifteen in 1847; she had spent most of her life in Concord. A tall, slender girl with a sad, handsome face, she wore her masses of glossy chestnut-colored hair piled around her head. Her feelings for Thoreau were balanced by a crush on the distant, learned Emerson, whose library had become one of her favorite haunts. One day, she picked up a translation of Bettina von Arnim's *Goethe's Corre-spondence with a Child,* the steamy story of an erotic connection between a fifteen-year-old and the older Goethe.

Although Emerson seemed responsive to Louisa the eager reader, she had picked the wrong Goethe in the businesslike older neighbor. In spite of his own experience to the contrary, Emerson believed that women didn't have a sexual component. They were chaste and lawful and put on earth to keep men in line. Louisa dropped off bunches of anonymous wildflowers at the Emersons' door, and Emerson pretended that he didn't know who had sent them. For the first time in her life, Louisa had her own room at Hillside, but privacy was at a premium in the Alcott family.

But Bronson felt unappreciated in Concord, and Emerson didn't feel like buying him another ticket to London. In October of 1848, the Alcotts moved back to Boston, taking dingy rooms in Dedham Street so that Bronson could hold Conversations and teach in rooms above Elizabeth Peabody's bookshop at 14 West Street. Louisa went from picking apples and baking in the kitchen in view of the apple trees outside the window to working in an urban basement kitchen where the principal view was of other people's passing feet.

The Alcotts' perpetual poverty had many results, but one of the most lasting was their impermanence, their being at the mercy of any uncle who decided to proffer charity or anyone who offered one of their daughters a job. In the decade between the years when they left Hillside, letting it out for rental, from the time they returned to Concord—by which time Hillside had been sold to Nathaniel Hawthorne, who rebuilt it—the family moved at least eight times. After the apartment on Dedham Street, they went to live for a few comfortable months with Abba's uncle in his big house on Atkinson Street as guests. Then they took rooms in Groton Street, after which they moved to 50 High Street.

From there, Louisa went to Dedham to work as a companion, a miserable job that lasted seven weeks. When she came home, the family had moved again. Enriched by the money from the sale to Hawthorne, they rented rooms on Beacon Hill, the newly chic part of town near the State House with views of the harbor, at 20 Pinckney Street. Soon enough, they were out of money again, so the whole family loaded up all their possessions and moved to Walpole, New Hampshire, where they once again tried to start a small school.

31

LOUISA IN BOSTON

———◆———

In many ways, the decade in Boston was Louisa May Alcott's coming of age. She didn't get married or even have real prospects. Instead, everyone in the Alcott family spent almost all their time just trying to survive. It was true that poor girls sometimes got married, but Louisa was in the odd position of being from a good family—her grandfather had been a colonel in the Revolution—but having no money for the kinds of things that men seemed to be attracted to.

She didn't play the pianoforte or sing, and anyway the family couldn't afford a piano. She would rather play a pirate in a play she had written than learn to embroider or draw as women were supposed to do. As for clothes, although she longed to buy the pretty things in the city's shopwindows or the tiny shoes and shawls, hats and dresses she saw sometimes on the Boston Common, the forty-five pounds of crinolines and underwear combined with cinched waists and bonnets that many fashionable women wore were both expensive and hopelessly impractical. More and more, writing and teaching seemed to be the only things she knew how to do.

In the barn at Hillside, Louisa had started putting on a few dramatic productions, and trapped in Boston without a teaching job, she began to write and eventually publish. Her first poem, published under the pseudonym Flora Fairchild, appeared in the *Saturday Evening Gazette*. She then published a book, *Flower Fables*, stories she had originally told young Ellen Emerson, the Emersons' daughter, back in what seemed the wonderful Concord days. The Alcotts' circumstances were so desperate that the tiny payments Louisa got—five or ten dollars—made a huge difference in their lives, and she decided all over again that she would become a writer. But Louisa took her family's financial needs far more seriously than her father did. So her decision to be a writer was hedged by the knowledge that she would take almost any job for money.

In February, pushed forward by her father's return from yet another financially disastrous tour as a lecturer in the American West, she wrote the story of her unhappy sojourn in Dedham as a maid of all work and took it to James Fields, the very man who had just published Nathaniel Hawthorne's *The Scarlet Letter.* Louisa heard that Fields had found the novel in a drawer and persuaded Hawthorne to let him have it—a typical apocryphal story about the genesis of a great book. Louisa had devoured Hawthorne's book, and she imagined that Fields would understand her as the book seemed to.

With her manuscript in hand, she made her way to the back of the Old Corner Bookstore, the center of Boston's literary life, where writers and would-be writers chatted while they waited for a word with the great one. Fields waved her to his desk while his young assistant Thomas Niles shuffled piles of other manuscripts. Years later, Thomas Niles would become Louisa's editor, and the force of his persuasion and her family's poverty would push her into writing a different book, a book she did not want to write. Now, in painful suspense over a book she had wanted very much to write, Louisa waited for the verdict on her first long piece. Would she be a writer? Could she publish a book? "Stick with your teaching," the great Fields said as Thomas Niles looked on. "You can't write."

Devastated, Louisa walked home to Pinckney Street. Her heart sank. Teaching possibilities seemed to be fewer and fewer. She couldn't bear household work. As she had written, her time as a companion in Dedham had been miserable and had showed her how brutally a family companion could be used when the man who hired her began to make advances—but only after forcing her to spend hours listening to his abysmal poetry and prose writing. She didn't know which was worse, praise she was expected to lavish on his mediocre talents, or the prospect of being sexually molested. Boston around her seemed to reflect her turmoil.

Back in Concord, she had helped her father and Henry David

Thoreau as they assisted slaves traveling north on the Underground Railroad. In Boston, this was not so simple. After the passage of the Fugitive Slave Act in 1850—which decreed that slaves must be returned to their owners even if they had escaped to states where slavery was illegal, like Massachusetts—harboring slaves or helping them to safety became more dangerous and more difficult.

In May of 1850, Shadrach Minkins, a slave who had escaped from his owner in Norfolk, Virginia, traveled to Boston by sea and found work as a waiter. He was arrested under the Fugitive Slave Act and given a hearing at the Boston Court House. Hearing that Shadrach had been arrested, a well-organized gang of African-Americans burst into the courthouse, freed Shadrach, and protected him as he escaped from Boston and into the Underground Railroad to Canada. After Shadrach was freed, the Boston Vigilance Committee was formed by citizens who wanted to support the cause, including Bronson Alcott. Nevertheless, in June, in spite of attempts to free him by force, another slave, Anthony Burns, was captured, made the subject of a hearing, and returned to his owner.

Even in Boston, there were those like Daniel Webster who believed that the law was the law and that it was everyone's obligation to return slaves to their owners, while men like William Lloyd Garrison furiously argued the opposite. Louisa had seen tremendous growth in Boston just in the few years since the Alcotts had moved to Dedham Street. It was becoming clear that the Alcotts' furious beliefs in individual liberty no matter what the color of a man's skin, although shared by Thoreau and eventually Emerson, were not shared by many of their countrymen. The Civil War was a long way off and right on the horizon at the same time. To her amazement, Louisa began to see that some people believed in the perpetuation of slavery, the necessity of slavery, in a way that was not going to change.

Others were so convinced that slavery was wrong that they would happily resort to violence to see slave laws overthrown and slaves illegally freed. Then there were those who would happily resort to violence just to make a point.

In November of 1852, Nathaniel Hawthorne's friend Franklin Pierce, a politician who had avoided having an opinion on the slavery issue, was elected president of the United States, helped along by

Hawthorne's campaign biography. The prohibition movement that had started in Maine the year before was beginning to spread, and Massachusetts enacted a law requiring children between the ages of eight and fourteen to attend school for at least twelve weeks a year. Over in England, one of Louisa's favorite writers, Charles Dickens, published his novel *Bleak House*. In Boston, the public library was founded. Harvard and Yale crews held their first rowing race, in New Hampshire on a two-mile course at Lake Winnepesaukee. Harvard won.

As for women, the seeds planted by Margaret Fuller had flowered in the Seneca Falls Convention in 1848, and at the close of the Anti-Slavery Convention in Boston, the members stayed on to discuss a national women's convention. The role of women in the 1840s and '50s was almost as hard to imagine as the role of African-Americans. Most agreed that in marriage—women's proper state—a woman essentially became her husband's possession. Bronson Alcott, who went to an 1853 women's convention, came back unimpressed.

By the summer of 1857, the Alcott family, beset with debts and once again feeling that a move might cure everything, decided to leave Walpole, New Hampshire. The house in Walpole had been leaky and crumbling. No one liked it. Worse, Lizzie, the second-youngest Alcott and the quietest, had become ill with what seemed to be recurring symptoms from an earlier bout with scarlet fever. Bronson thought of moving to Malden, Massachusetts, to build a new house. The family considered a return to Boston. But the eternal Alcott question remained: where would the money come from?

32

CONCORD AGAIN

———◆———

Bronson decided that he was homesick for Concord and that he would never be happy unless he could return to Concord. Lizzie also wanted to return to Concord, the village where she had been a carefree, healthy young girl. As it turned out, John Moore's dilapidated brown clapboard house on the Lexington Road was available for purchase. The house included ten acres of butternut and elm trees, lumber for keeping the house warm in the winter, a good well and a sound cellar, as well as an orchard of forty apple trees that produced an annual twenty-barrel crop.

The small-windowed house featured a huge elm in the front next to a path leading to the Lexington Road, and sloping land that reached steeply behind it. It was a familiar landscape, since the Alcotts' old Concord house, which they had called Hillside when they bought it as a pig farm from Horatio Cogswell, was right next door. Hillside was now named Wayside and owned by the Hawthornes, but since Nathaniel and Sophia were in England, Sophia's father, Dr. Peabody, was temporarily living there. After his death at the age of ninety, he would be succeeded as a tenant by Sophia's sister Mary, who was recovering from the death of her husband Horace Mann. Across the street and a little ways toward town was the Emerson House, with its respectable white porch, its well-kept lawns sloping down to the brook, its interesting library, and its endless supply of conversation and visits with great men.

The Moore house was on the market for $950. Emerson as usual paid $500, and the remaining $450 came from a collection taken up among the family friends. Abba's father wrote a check to cover the debts they were leaving behind in Walpole. For once, Bronson spared his family the usual lecture about his principles preventing him from buying property. More and more, this lecture sounded like a bad excuse for taking other people's money. Instead, he set to work with the help of Thoreau and anyone else he could find to make the Moore place habitable.

What was habitable to a family like the Alcotts in the 1850s would be far from habitable for most Americans today. They had no running water or central heat or refrigeration. Water was pumped from a well and carried, food was kept in cupboards, and there was no indoor plumbing. In the meantime, during the renovations, the family rented half a house near the railroad station in Concord.

It was hard for Louisa to return to Concord after the years of adventure and trials and tribulations and the feeling of being the center of things that she had in Boston. The little village seemed hardly changed, and there was something stultifying about coming back. Her doubts about the family's new house were quickly subsumed by her anxiety about her sister. As she sickened, Lizzie wasted away, and the pain seemed to drive her mad. Abba, who had brought the scarlet fever home with her from working with charity cases in Boston, was racked with guilt. Even on large doses of opium, Lizzie attacked her sisters and asked to be left in peace. Always a loving, meek girl, she now lashed out at everything around her. She hated it; she hated it all.

Louisa sat with her sister day and night, carrying her up and down stairs, bathing her and keeping her warm with a fire. By the first days of March, it was clear that Lizzie was failing, and early one morning, with Louisa and Abba by her bed, she finally stopped breathing. Both saw a light mist leave her body and rise up into the air. The wasted twenty-three-year-old was buried in Sleepy Hollow, not far from the center of town.

Then a few weeks later, Louisa's older sister Anna, twenty-seven, decided to accept the proposal of John Pratt. Pratt, who sometimes played the Dutch peasant in the Alcott family theatricals, was an insurance salesman who had courted Anna with visits to his family farm. Louisa felt that she was losing everything, first Lizzie and now Anna.

Anna's departure felt like betrayal; she was choosing to leave the family in order to get married, and it also threw Louisa's single state into sharp relief.

In the spring, the family—or what was left of it—finally moved into the brown clapboard house they called Orchard House, and decorated it with the busts of Socrates and Plato, the globe, and the books, the Murillo engraving of the Virgin with the moon under her feet, and the pieces of furniture that had traveled with them for so long. Abby chose a little room over the back porch where a grapevine grew across the window and set up her painting studio. Louisa moved in next to her in the front of the house with her half-moon desk, her marble paperweight and leather portfolio. Out her windows on either side of the desk she could see through the branches of the elm to the road and beyond to the meadows sloping down the ridge. " 'Tis a pretty retreat," wrote Bronson, always the optimist, especially when his own talents and someone else's money were involved. "And ours; a family mansion to take pride in, rescued as it is from deformity and disgrace by those touches of grace and plain-keeping which I have contrived to give it."

With his eternally renewable pride of hearth, Bronson set to work restoring and repairing on the inside and planting trees on the outside. He built a rambling rail fence in which he used, the carpenter said, as many nails as would ordinarily be used to build a house, but it was charming and very much an Alcott fence. Inside it, he built a rustic round bench fitted to the trunk of the giant elm tree where he could sit in the afternoon and watch the world go by.

Bronson immediately took up with his old friends, and on Monday afternoons the family parlor swelled with visitors—students from Frank Sanborn's nearby school and Thoreau with a new sapling to be planted behind the house or Mr. Emerson with a book he thought Louisa might like to read.

33

WALDEN, *WALDEN*

———◆———

Henry David Thoreau didn't write *Walden* at Walden. He built his small shingle cottage in the woods with the intention of writing a book about his brother John and their trip north in the *Musketaquid*. They started in the Sudbury River just past the Old South Bridge and sailed, paddled, dragged, and sometimes carried the boat with its small wheels about fifty-five miles north as far as Hooksett, New Hampshire. The day the brothers left town was a rainy day, so they delayed their departure until the afternoon. They fired their guns to signal their departure. They paddled up to Billerica, where they spent their first night, through the locks into the Merrimack River with its rapids and broad ponds, to a campsite below the Tyngsboro Ferry, past Nashua at the mouth of the Penichook, past the Amoskeag Falls, through the locks at Cromwell's Falls, past Thornton's Ferry and Naticook Brook, past Coos Falls and Goff's Falls, and to Hooksett. At Hooksett, the brothers hid their boat in the mouth of a small stream and continued north on foot and by stagecoach into the White Mountains even farther than Concord, New Hampshire. A week later, they returned, uncovered the boat, and started back down the river to Concord, Massachusetts. The Thoreaus had "come away up here among the hills to learn the impartial and unbribeable beneficence of nature," Thoreau wrote. It was a tense time in their close relationship. They were both in love with the same woman, a topic they did not discuss. They had also come away to show their loyalty to each other.

A Week on the Concord and Merrimack Rivers was the book

Thoreau intended to write, and he did, although the account of the brothers' adventure is suffused with the sadness of loss, the sense of John, who had been dead almost five years. Thoreau couldn't find a publisher for the book; he paid the cost of printing 1,000 copies himself. He sold fewer than 300 copies and finally stored the remainder in his parents' Concord attic. He joked that he was in possession of a large library, mostly written by himself. Not until the summer of 1854, almost a decade after it was written, did Ticknor & Fields, with absolutely no enthusiasm, agree to publish *Walden,* the book Thoreau had based on his experiences during his two years of living on Walden Pond. Although it hardly seemed possible, *Walden* actually did not do as well as Thoreau's previous abysmal failure. It earned nothing. "In his declining months Thoreau had constantly to face the crushing reality of his failure, to reconcile himself to oblivion," writes Perry Miller. "The world decided . . . that he would figure as a minor naturalist in a literature where the giants were Irving, Longfellow, Lowell and Dr. Holmes."

At Walden Pond, happily innocent of his grim immediate future as a writer, and unhappily innocent of his brilliant distant future, Thoreau found a freedom in writing that had eluded him before. He set to work on *A Week,* but at the same time his journals became increasingly candid and increasingly angry.

For years, Thoreau had lived in poverty on other people's handouts. He was sick to death of it. "Be sure that you give the poor the aid they most need," he wrote in a paragraph which might have been directed at Emerson. "If you give money, spend yourself with it, and do not merely abandon it to them. . . . Often the poor man is not so cold and hungry as he is dirty and ragged and gross. It is partly his taste and not merely his misfortune." Emerson with his grand house, his important connections, his money and his ability to reel in his wife if she strayed too far from his own convenience, had not been an easy patron.

Although he had retired to Walden, Thoreau was not a hermit. He regularly walked to town, and in February gave a lecture at the Concord Lyceum on the subject of Thomas Carlyle, the Scottish writer who had influenced Emerson so much. The lecture went well, but it was the question-and-answer period that changed Thoreau's life. No one asked about Carlyle; question after question came about Thoreau himself. Why had he decided to live in the woods? What was it like out there? Why had he left town? More or less by popular demand, Thoreau started making notes for a series of lectures that he titled "Walden, or Life in the Woods."

Freed from his daily indebtedness to Emerson, he wrote as if awakening, and the sense of awakening runs through the book. *Walden* is the first American memoir, the first book in which the days and nights of an autobiographical, confessional narrator are the central plotline. Thoreau invented nature writing and memoir writing in one swift, brilliant stroke. It was Emerson's land, but it was Thoreau's house— for the first time his own house, for the first time his own garden, for the first time his own desk and chair. "My furniture, part of which I made myself . . . consisted of a bed, a table, a desk, three chairs, a looking glass three inches in diameter, a pair of tongs and andirons, a kettle, a skillet, and a frying-pan, a dipper, a wash-bowl, two knives and forks, three plates, one cup, one spoon, a jug for oil, a jug for molasses and a japanned lamp. None is so poor that he need sit on a pumpkin," he wrote proudly.

Thoreau felt the way the landscape feels on a warm day at the end of March. Piles of snow are melting, the ground has long patches of cobwebby ice, but there is the first mud of spring, and everywhere the sound of running water as the world begins to relax and thaw. The first ducks swim in the watery places where the ice has gone. Others fly and skid to a stop feet-first at the edges of the pond where the reeds are suddenly slightly green. Under the clear green surface of the water, the plants at the bottom are beginning to sway in the current. The earth looks rich, and in the deepest woods tiny green shoots almost imperceptibly find their way through the surface. Earthworms crawl across the paths where the tracks of deer and rabbits and sometimes a wild turkey are suddenly clear.

In all this freedom, Thoreau was increasingly furious. "I have thus a tight shingled and plastered house, ten feet wide by fifteen long, and eight feet posts, with a garret and a closet, a large window on each side, two trap doors, one door at the end, and a brick fireplace opposite." The exact cost of the house alone, as Thoreau shows in his careful accounting, was 28 dollars, 12½ cents. "Towers and temples are the luxury of princes. A simple and independent mind does not toil at the bidding of any prince. Genius is not a retainer to any emperor," he wrote. "As for the pyramids, there is nothing to wonder at in them so much as the fact that so many men could be found degraded enough to spend their lives constructing a tomb for some ambitious booby, whom it would have been wiser and manlier to have drowned in the Nile and then given his body to the dogs."

34

THOREAU NOW

———◆———

We revere Thoreau for his contempt for material things. We love him for damning new clothes and cautioning us against possessions. We like his judgment that other men and women are leading lives of quiet desperation. He ran a farm and built a house with outbuildings for $36.78, according to his accounting. "Nothing was given to me of which I have not rendered some account." But we love him because we are swamped with things, because even the simplest of us could not list our possessions in a few lines or even a few pages. In a world where materialism has eclipsed religion, Thoreau's messages have a different ring than they did in a world where religion was changing and materials were few. Thoreau was certainly a prophet without honor in his own time, but times had to change for his prophesies to have the weight and wit they have today.

Thoreau had very little in a community which had little. His first chapter, "Economy," is a raging screed against the rich and their attachment to their money and their idiotic attitude toward those who have less. "There is no odor so bad as that which arises from goodness tainted. . . . If I knew for a certainty that a man was coming to my house with the conscious design of doing me good, I should run for my life, as from that dry and parching wind of the African deserts called the simoon, which fills the mouth and nose and ears and eyes with dust till you are suffocated, for fear that I should get some of his good done to me,—some of its virus mingled in my blood." No wonder Emerson didn't often take the pleasant walk under the great elms down the Cambridge Turnpike to see his old friend at Walden Pond.

Walden is a masterpiece, but it is generally cited more than it is read. The mention of *Walden* in polite society inevitably elicits great praise. "My favorite book," someone says. Or "I live by that book." What they mean is that they know about the book and take it to be a handbook for the simpler life they might want to lead, if they ever got tired of making money and going to parties, or if they ever came to believe that the status in their community that makes them comfortable was really not important at all. They remember a few of the aphorisms often excerpted: Beware of all enterprises that require new clothes, for instance. Or simplify, simplify, simplify. They haven't read the book itself, and perhaps that's just as well. Thoreau is not kind to the rich or even the middle class. He also advances some of the most brilliant arguments for being a vegetarian and for abstaining from drinking that have ever been written.

"The practical objection to animal food in my case was its uncleanness; and besides, when I had caught and cleaned and cooked and eaten my fish, they seemed not to have fed me essentially. It was insignificant and unnecessary and cost more than it came to. A little bread or a few potatoes would have done as well with less trouble and filth." After calling freshly caught fish filth, he launches into a defense of drinking only water. "I would fain keep sober always; and there are infinite degrees of drunkenness. I believe that water is the only drink for a wise man; wine is not so noble a liquor; and think of dashing the hopes of a morning with a cup of warm coffee. . . . Of all ebriosity, who does not prefer to be intoxicated by the air he breathes?"

A day at Walden often started early, as the rising sun dyed the world a bright pink. In the summer, Thoreau would sometimes swim in the pond that lay before him; in the winter, he would start a fire and warm himself as the morning train from Boston to Concord rattled by on the tracks next to the pond. Mornings, he read or wrote in his journal or worked on his book. Thoreau ate little. A piece of bread dipped in honey was his idea of a meal, and if he also had an apple or some beans, it was a feast. In the afternoons, if he didn't walk the mile into town to visit the Emersons, or his mother or another friend, he would sometimes go fishing off his boat, or play the flute.

Thoreau's retirement from the community was not meant to be a social retirement. The truth was that he needed a place to live. Even when he didn't go into town, he ran into the Irish families who were still around Concord from having worked on the railroad, or other people who had come out to Walden to fish or swim. In the evening, the bullfrogs would start up in the marshes at the edge of the pond, and as the last train to Boston went past, its windows lighted up from inside, the fireflies came out and he could hear carriages rumbling over wooden bridges to the east and the lowing of someone's cattle and the barking of a far-off dog. Some evenings, a flock of geese would come honking into the pond for a noisy landing just as night fell.

When Thoreau didn't entertain visitors, he was in town, as much a walker in the streets that ran off the Main Street over the Milldam as he was when he was living there with his family. He continued to advise his father about the pencil factory and about the new house into which the Thoreau family had moved. He called on the Emersons and played with Eddie and Edith or chatted with Lidian if her husband was away. He dropped in on the Alcotts at Hillside, helping to tutor the youngest girls and talking with Louisa, who was always the most serious of the family and who always had some questions for him.

35

LEAVING WALDEN

———◆———

On September 6, 1847, Thoreau left Walden and moved back into his father's house in the village. "I left the woods for as good a reason as I went there," he wrote. "Perhaps it seemed to me that I had several more lives to live, and could not spare any time for that one." But as Thoreau's life unfolded and he moved back into the Emerson House for a harmonious two years, he often looked back with nostalgia. "Why did I leave the woods?" he wrote in his journal a few years later. "I do not think I can tell. I do not know any better how I came to go there. I have often wished myself back. Perhaps I wanted change. There was a little stagnation, it may be, about two 'o clock in the afternoon. Perhaps if I lived there much longer I might have lived there forever. One might think twice before he accepted heaven on such terms."

Leaving Walden seemed to propel Thoreau out into the world. As a traveler, he nearly always walked, carrying his few possessions in a folded-up handkerchief or a little folded paper. He dressed simply, an affectation which was extremely eccentric in a world where even ordinary women spent hours dressing their hair into complicated buns and braids and at least three layers of clothing were required of men and women for the simplest outing. As a writer, the next seven years of his life would be principally devoted to rewriting the manuscript of the journals he had kept at Walden and looking for a publisher. In the meantime, he published his piece about climbing in Maine titled *Ktaadn* after Mount Katahdin, as well as *A Week on the Concord and*

Merrimack Rivers and *Resistance to Civil Government,* all in 1849, and the first four chapters of *Cape Cod,* in 1852.

Because it took so long to get *Walden* published, Thoreau had time to rewrite two years of his journals into one of the most magnificent books in English. Two years of notes became one year; digressions were reined in and brought forward in time. Sentences were worked and reworked. There is something heroic and obsessive about the way Thoreau went about making his manuscript of *Walden* perfect. He seemed to know how important it was. He expanded the natural descriptions, and took out some of the personal discomforts. In 1852, he completed the fourth draft of the manuscript. In 1853, he completed the fifth draft, with 112 new pages. In January 1854, he completed a seventh draft, adding another 46 pages. In April that year, he was correcting printer's proofs. The book was finally published in August of 1854, and although its sales were tiny, it got Thoreau a great deal of attention in the Concord community.

His timing was perfect in a small way. The country was just far enough from wilderness to begin the love affair with nature with a capital *N* that is still going on today. In New York, Olmsted and Vaux were designing the delicious "natural" landscape of dells and rambles that is Central Park. It was also a great year for literature. In England, Alfred Lord Tennyson published "The Charge of the Light Brigade," the memoirs of Isaac Newton were published, Charles Dickens published *Hard Times.*

What creates a masterpiece? In the case of *The Scarlet Letter* and *Walden,* both arguably the finest works of two men whom we now regard as great writers, the impetus seems to have come from a sharp despair. Both men felt, as they began to write, that they had nothing more to lose. Hawthorne had lost his job, his mother, his hometown; Thoreau had lost his brother and the prospect of anyplace to live besides a homemade hut on borrowed land. There is a fearlessness about both these books, an honesty about the human heart, with its petty angers and dreadful fears, that neither writer found again.

Naturally, having finally completed *Walden,* Thoreau wasn't sure about his next book. He researched a book about the Indians and started work, but he was also tempted by the prospect of writing a biography of the maverick slavery fighter John Brown. Brown hadn't visited Concord yet, but the conviction of the Transcendentalists was already in place when it came to the subject of the slaves. As far as Thoreau and Alcott and eventually Emerson were concerned, this was an issue that did not have two sides, and it's interesting to see how these extraordinarily moral men helped lead their beloved country into a dreadful quagmire of war and loss. As the years progressed, counting down to the firing on Fort Sumter, which almost seemed like a casual accident—the men who fired had been at West Point with the men they fired on—passion in Concord grew more and more heated and less and less rational.

For the men of Concord and their counterparts in Boston, the controversy was not over states' rights or the preservation of the union, it was over the fate of the frightened, downtrodden people who had been treated like possessions, auctioned off as if they were less important than furniture, and separated from their own families at the whim of their owners. Slaves had been used in ways that even animals were never used. This was wrong. The politicians in Washington did not agree with the thinkers in Concord. Few politicians cared about the plight of the slaves. As the Civil War approached, it became clear that for the new president, Abraham Lincoln, the slaves were less important than the preservation of the Union.

Like most men of the 1860s, Lincoln could not imagine a world in which the former slaves might mix with white gentlewomen and gentlemen as if they were equal. He carefully reassured the southern states in many speeches, explaining that he had no desire to do away with slavery. "If I could save the Union without freeing any slave, I would do it," Lincoln wrote to Horace Greeley, "and if I could save it by freeing all the slaves, I would do it; and if I could do it by freeing some and leaving others alone I would also do that."

For him and the Senate, the issue was the coming apart of the United States, not the desperate situation of the slaves. Many people— including Nathaniel Hawthorne—thought that the institution of slavery would just fade away as the South became more prosperous. Others, in England, believed the answer was to compensate the slaveholders for the loss of their "property" as the British had done.

In Concord, though, the issue of slavery became intensely personal. Everyone in town had seen the runaways, and the Alcott house had become a stop on the Underground Railroad. The Peabody sisters were on fire for the cause of the downtrodden, and while the Hawthornes were in England, their house had also been used by Mary and Elizabeth as a hiding place. Thoreau was one of the men who took the runaways to the railroad station and bought their tickets to Canada, with money from Emerson, of course.

For the Alcotts, Thoreau, and Emerson, slavery was not some far-off, economically questionable institution, it was the scared faces of the men and women and sometimes children they had fed and harbored and helped—or, in the case of Anthony Burns, been unable to help. Thoreau's belief that slavery was wrong was based on his own vivid experience with the suffering of others, and it made him uncompromising and angry. Personal experience often has this effect. Once we've seen the suffering of others, once we've been forced to acknowledge their humanity, it's hard to go back to being political, to being able to negotiate and compromise.

Working to register black voters in Mississippi and Alabama in the 1960s created a generation of northerners who were unable to see both sides on the question of the southern character. Are there two sides? Are the white residents of those small southern towns really beyond redemption? Working with the homeless in a shelter changes the attitudes of the workers, just as working in a rape crisis center changes the attitude of those who work there.

Personal experience is the lightning of the soul; it transforms the heart in ways that leave the brain behind. It was this division between those who took slavery to heart like Thoreau and Alcott, Louisa May Alcott, Franklin Sanborn, and finally Emerson, and those who struggled to find a solution to the impending war through political negotiation like Hawthorne and Lincoln, which would help tear the Concord community apart as the war approached. For those who had sheltered the frightened and fed the hungry, there could be no compromise; for those who saw the Union coming apart, there could only be compromise.

It was this inability to step back and become political that shattered the community Emerson had built with his first wife's money. "If Transcendentalism did not remain a disturbing force, the reason is not alone that Americans adopted it and made it orthodox," writes Perry

Miller in the introduction to his book *The Transcendentalists,* "but also that it consumed, shattered and destroyed its adherents. Margaret Fuller fled to Europe to violence and to death. . . . Parker killed himself with overwork and Thoreau expended himself; Emerson dissolved into aphasia, Ripley subsided into disillusion, Hedge became a Harvard professor. . . . Elizabeth Peabody became a 'character.' . . . Ellery Channing spent a life of futility. Bronson Alcott alone endured . . . but he lived a life of meditative leisure shamelessly parasitic on the labors of his wife and daughters." Of course, one of those daughters, Louisa May, also survived not only as a witness to Transcendentalism but as a believer herself, leading a life that began as a student of Thoreau's and ended with her paying for everyone and everything as Emerson had before her.

36

THE BIRTH AND DEATH OF
MARGARET FULLER

◆

In the cause of the Roman Revolution, Margaret Fuller seemed to find her place in a life of indignation and protest against injustice. Trying to establish a democracy and a separate Roman Republic, a city that would no longer harbor the pope or be the center of the Catholic Church, the Romans were furiously opposed by the French Army and the Austrian Army, who needed their ranks of Italian Catholics. From today's perspective, a united Italy seems a foregone conclusion. In 1848, it was as fiercely opposed as the cause of the South's secession from the United States would be opposed a few years later.

The cause, led by the romantic revolutionary Giuseppe Garibaldi—a government for the people and by the people—was clear, and made clearer for Fuller by her passionate friendships with Italian revolutionaries and her affair with Giovanni Ossoli.

In July of 1849, the French occupied Rome and Garibaldi was forced to retreat to Venice. "I know that many 'respectable' gentlemen would be surprised to hear me speak in this way," Fuller wrote as a foreign correspondent in her last dispatch to the *Tribune,* after giving a romantic, adoring description of Garibaldi leaving Rome. "Gentlemen who perform their 'duties to society' by buying for themselves handsome clothes and furniture with the interest of their money, speak of Garibaldi and his men as 'brigands' and 'vagabonds.' Such they are, doubtless in the same way that Jesus, Eneas and Moses were."

Fuller, a spinster nearing the age of forty, would have been condemned to a narrow, empty life back in her native Massachusetts. In Italy, she found life rich and filled with new challenges that sometimes seemed to overwhelm her. In Rome, she worked in a hospital on the Quirinal Hill caring for wounded soldiers during her pregnancy, a pregnancy complicated by her age. Only when she had to because of her advanced pregnancy did she leave Rome for the small mountain town of Rieti to give birth to her child. Caught between her political convictions, her desire to be on the front lines, and her powerful maternal instincts, Fuller first left the baby in Rieti to go to Rome and work in the hospital, and then hurriedly returned.

The conflict between her child and her work was hard. "I have enjoyed many bright peaceful hours this winter," she wrote a friend. "My little baby flourishes in my care; his laughing eyes, his stammered words and capricious caresses afford me the most unalloyed quiet joy I have ever known." In spite of her fears about the restrictions of life as a couple and her disdain for the "jog trot of domestic life," she also enjoyed being with Ossoli.

"He is not in any respect such a person as people would expect to find with me," she wrote her mother back in Groton, "he has had no instructor except an old priest who entirely neglected his education. . . . His love for me has been unswerving and most tender. . . . In him I have found a home. . . ." Her letters to Emerson tell a slightly different story and never mention Ossoli or the baby. After a long description of the battle to retake Rome and the scene in the hospital, she wrote, "Should I never return,—and sometimes I despair of doing so, it seems so far off so difficult and I am caught in such a net of ties here,—if ever you know of my life here, I think you will only wonder at the constancy with which I have sustained myself. . . . Meanwhile love me all you can; let me feel, that, amid the fearful agitations of the world, there are pure hands, with healthful even pulse, stretched out toward me, if I claim their grasp."

Rome was lost, and in the summer of 1849, Fuller, Ossoli, and their baby retreated to settle in Florence. Life in Florence was calmer; here there were no flying bullets, nighttime bombardments, or massing troops. Ossoli started taking sculpture classes, while Margaret was able to devote herself to their baby and to working on her history of the

Roman Revolution for which she had high hopes. She visited friends like Elizabeth Barrett Browning and her husband.

Even in a peaceful city, Margaret saw the future as bleak and frightening. Ossoli's conservative family, upset by his revolutionary activities and his unlegalized connection with the Protestant Fuller, cut him off financially. Fuller would have to find a way to support her family, and in Italy that was impossible. On the other hand, returning home with Ossoli and the baby was a terrifying prospect. Margaret as a single woman had plenty of social difficulty; Margaret as a mother with an Italian husband didn't even bear thinking about. Sometimes both choices seemed impossible, and at those times Margaret seemed to have some premonitions of doom. "For me, I long so very much to see you," she wrote her mother, who had welcomed the idea of Ossoli and the baby in a happy letter months earlier; "should anything hinder it on earth again (and I say it merely because there seems so much more danger on sea than on land) think of your daughter as one who always wished at least to do her duty, and who always cherished you according as her mind opened to discover excellence."

The baby was all joy. "He is now in the most perfect, rosy health, a very gay impetuous, ardent but sweet tempered child," she wrote proudly. The future was all despair. As she made plans for her family's trip back to the United States, for financial reasons Fuller chose to sail from Italy and ignore even Emerson's offers of help in buying a ticket. She booked a passage on the bark *Elizabeth* out of Leghorn—in Italian, Livorno. As the sailing date of May 19 approached, Margaret became more and more terrified. "Rainy weather delays us now from day to day," she wrote her Florence friends Emlyn and William Story, "as our ship the *Elizabeth* (look out for news of shipwreck) cannot finish taking on her cargo till come one or two good days."

In spite of her faith in the *Elizabeth*'s captain, New Englander Seth Hasty, Margaret was filled with foreboding. The *Elizabeth* had been loaded up with tons of Carrara marble, including a statue of Senator John C. Calhoun carved in Italy and headed for the statehouse in Columbia, South Carolina, and she was riding low in the water already. Robert Browning visited the boat as Fuller began to load her possessions aboard and advised her not to go. She wrote another friend that she would embark, "praying indeed fervently, that it may not be my lot to lose my babe at sea, either by unsolaced sickness, or amid the howling waves; or that if I should it may be brief anguish, and Ossoli, he and I go together."

Margaret's foreboding began to seem prescient almost immediately. By June 2, a week after sailing, as the ship *Elizabeth* left Gibraltar and tacked out of the friendly Mediterranean Sea into the unpredictable Atlantic, the admired Captain Seth Hasty contracted smallpox. He quickly worsened and died and was summarily buried at sea. Then the beloved baby Angelino, called Nino, also contracted smallpox. Terrified that he might die, in a maternal panic that he might bear ugly scars that would influence her family and friends' reaction to him in Boston, Margaret nursed the baby day and night. As the ship bumped across the ocean going west, she and Ossoli were able to bring their child through the disease and restore him to robust, adorable health. Fuller breathed a sigh of relief.

Point O' Woods, to which *Elizabeth* was headed, is one of this country's most exclusive beach communities; it is bordered by a chain-link fence that separates it from the more raffish Fire Island community of Ocean Bay Park, and the gate in the fence is usually locked. With its beach club and general store and its private ferry from the mainland, the little community is open only to those who own houses there, and as a result it has the pleasant, friendly feeling of an earlier age. People there can be hospitable and lovingly generous, but there is also the whisper of exclusion, the vision of the locked gate somewhere in the background.

37

SHIPWRECK

———◆———

As the *Elizabeth* finally approached New York on July 18, gale winds, so high that they shut down all local shipping, began to blow. Acting Captain Henry Bangs, the ship's inexperienced first mate, had no way of knowing the severity of the storm. In the confusion of wind and waves, he mistook the Fire Island Light for the Navesink Light in New Jersey. As they sailed unknowingly past their destination in New York Harbor east toward Fire Island, Bangs told the passengers they were just off Cape May. He ordered them to do their final packing to prepare for arrival in New York Harbor the next day.

At about 2:30 A.M. on the night of July 19, Bangs got up to take a sounding. The wind and waves seemed to toss the little boat around like a toy. The plumb line showed that at least they were in deep water, there was no danger of running aground, and he went back to bed. Then at 3:30 A.M. the *Elizabeth* hit the Fire Island sandbar just off Point O' Woods. The passengers were awakened by the sickening crunch of wood against sand. A wave lifted the boat up and crashed her stern back down onto the bar, where she stuck as her cargo of heavy marble blocks began breaking out through the wooden hull. Separated from her husband in the confusion of the shipwreck, Margaret stumbled from the flooding cabins up to the forecastle. There she comforted her baby son and refused to abandon the ship or her position.

Huddled together in the howling rain and wind, the captain's widow, Fuller, her baby, and a few of the crew waited for dawn, when they saw how close they were to land. The beach was right there on the other side of what seemed like an infinity of roiling water. The lifeboats had been splintered by the crash, and Fuller gave her life preserver to a crewman with the idea that he would bring out a rescue boat. Out past the shoreline, just where the surfers today like to slice the face of a wave, she sat wearing a white nightgown with her long dark hair streaming around her.

Volunteers from the American Shipwreck Society—an early version of the Coast Guard—arrived with a lifeboat and mortar, but because of the storm they were unable to launch the boat. The mortar—a 300-pound cannon with a 24-pound ball at the end of the rope that could be used to rescue passengers—kept falling short of the wreck. Fuller's friend Horace Sumner, who had also been a passenger on the *Elizabeth* and whose brother Charles was the famous senator from Massachusetts, jumped into the water and was swept under and drowned while they watched. The noise of the baby crying and other passengers weeping was drowned out by the wind and crashing waves. Others held onto planks or spars or hatch covers.

Finally, Fuller allowed a crew member to try to reach the shore with her infant son. The man had been a friend of Nino's throughout the voyage, he loved the cheerful little boy, and he rigged up a sling that held the baby to his wide chest. Margaret watched as he clutched her baby with one hand and grabbed a spar with the other and jumped off the boat. Both crewman and baby drowned. As the day wore on, the beach became crowded with rescuers and hundreds of scavengers who brought carts to make off with whatever they could find from the *Elizabeth*'s cargo of silks, oils, and Italian braid.

"We could see some of the crew on the deck, the others were on the forecastle," wrote a reporter for the *New York Tribune* who got to the beach at about 11 A.M., in time to watch the final hours of the 530-ton wooden bark. "The tide was rising and we could render them no assistance. We were in hopes that the ship could hold together till low water when there might be a chance of boarding her; but at about 2:30 'o clock the gale and the breakers both increased, and the ship began to break up, and in fifteen minutes not a vestige of her remained." All the passengers were lost; the only survivors were a dozen of the crew, including the captain's widow, who had leapt into the boiling ocean before the ship came apart.

Word of the tragedy reached Emerson's house in Concord, Massa-chusetts, three days later, and the devastated Emerson sent Henry David Thoreau to Point O' Woods to investigate. Fuller's desk, some papers, and some clothes had been washed up, but her body was not recovered. Thoreau returned to Concord with only a button from the coat of Fuller's husband, Count Giovanni Ossoli. "I have in my pocket a button which I ripped off the coat of the Marquis of Ossoli on the seashore the other day," he wrote. "Our thoughts are the epochs of our lives; all else is but as a journal of the winds that blew while we were here."

By the time Thoreau got to Fire Island, the sea was calm, and Lieu-tenant Francis Martin and the USS Revenue Cutter *Mohawk* had both been dispatched to unload what could be salvaged. Fuller's manuscript of her great book about the Roman Revolution was never found. The marble statue of John C. Calhoun was rescued, hauled out of the water, and shipped to South Carolina, where it was installed in the state house for which it had been ordered. It was destroyed during the Civil War when General Sherman's Army marched triumphantly through South Carolina.

Thoreau was haunted for the rest of his life by what he saw on the beach at Point O' Woods. In October of 1863, the *Atlantic Monthly* pub-lished his essay "Life Without Principle," another attack on the cor-ruptions of wealth and perhaps Thoreau's most eloquent call for a different kind of goal for human life than materialism. "I saw the other day, a vessel which had been wrecked, and many lives lost, and her cargo of rags, juniper berries, and bitter almonds were strewn along the shore. It seemed hardly worth the while to tempt the dangers of the sea between Leghorn and New York for the sake of a cargo of juniper berries and bitter almonds. America sending to the Old World for her bitters! Is not the sea-brine, is not shipwreck, bitter enough to make the cup of life go down here? Yet such, to a great extent, is our boasted commerce; and there are those who style themselves statesmen and philosophers who are so blind as to think that progress and civilization depend on precisely this kind of interchange and activity—the activity of flies about a molasses-hogshead."

Sophia Hawthorne and her husband got the awful news about the shipwreck after the friends in Concord. She heard from her friend Caroline Tappan, who handed her a pile of news clippings, as if the whole thing was too awful to discuss. It was a summer day, and the sun slanted across the meadows in front of the little red house. They had left Salem behind and they thought they had left Concord behind. Fuller was no longer a problem; her place in their marriage had been taken by the adorable Herman Melville. Hawthorne's thoughts on hearing of the death of his old friend have not survived. His little wife, though, could hardly keep herself from gloating.

"I dread to speak of Margaret," Sophia wrote. "Oh, was ever anything so tragical, so dreary, so unspeakably agonizing as the image of Margaret on that wreck alone." A little while later, the grieving Sophia recovered her composure and wrote in a moment of clarity. "I am really glad she died," Sophia confided to her mother-in-law back in Salem. "There was no other peace or rest to be found for her—especially if her husband was a person so wanting in force and availability." For Sophia, marriage to Hawthorne had been a kind of miracle. She had been called almost from the land of the dead into leading a useful and productive life. Her own admiration of Fuller took second place to the preservation of her new life as Mrs. Nathaniel Hawthorne.

In 1899, the women of Point O' Woods, led by Lillie Devereaux Blake and the New York City Woman Suffrage League, built a pergola at the edge of the dunes in memory of Fuller. Julia Ward Howe, author of the "Battle Hymn of the Republic," wrote an inscription citing Fuller's "uplifting influence." But in another storm in 1913, the pergola too was washed away by the sea.

The Point O' Woods town library, housed in a charming shingle house near the Great South Bay side of town, features some best-sellers and clippings about those who, over the years, have remembered the wreck of the *Elizabeth*. The doomed boat carrying Margaret Fuller and her family was not the only wreck to meet its fate on the sandbar that lurks just under the water at Fire Island's southern edge. In fact, Fire Island allegedly got its name from the great fires pirates built to lure unsuspecting ships onto the sand to be wrecked and plundered. In the little town post office, photographs of more recent wrecks on the same sandbar that broke the *Elizabeth* into bits show how close the boats are to the beach even as they fill up with water and sand. If only the wooden hold hadn't been filled with all that marble; if only, if only, if only.

The beach at night is spooky. It's 3:30 A.M., and my daughter and I, there to observe the moment the *Elizabeth* hit the sandbar on July 19th, stand at the dune line. We say an improvised prayer for the souls of all those lost at sea. As I walk down the beach toward the water, I'm amazed to see two sets of recent footprints in the sand heading toward the south where the Fire Island Light glows and then darkens and glows again in the mist. Looking out at the black water and the one fishing-boat light far out on the horizon, I can almost hear the dreadful crash as the *Elizabeth* hits the bar; almost feel the water rushing through the fragile hull. At night I have dreams of the dark water, the fear and confusion, the numbness that precedes drowning. The shipwreck was more than a century ago, but the ocean still pounds against the beach and the sandbar is out there waiting, just beneath the line of breakers.

38

THE HAWTHORNES'
RETURN TO CONCORD

———◆———

The Hawthornes were in Lenox when they got the awful news that Fuller, Ossoli, and their baby had been lost. After her heroic years in Italy, followed by her dreadful death, confusion about Fuller—who she was and how she should have been treated—haunted her friends. The dramatic circumstances of her death seemed to give her an overpowering presence that ruptured the balance of sexual attraction, intellectual stimulation, and distance that she had achieved with her friends while she was alive.

After Fuller's death, in page after page, novel after novel, Hawthorne described and redescribed situations of sexy feminine outcasts: that of the mother of the illegitimate child cast out by her own community, that of a woman who dies of drowning after being corrupted by the influence of a greater man, and that of a seductive woman in Rome suffering the confusions of being abroad. Fuller died in 1850; in the twelve years after that, during which Nathaniel Hawthorne wrote four extraordinary novels, she was memorialized and rememorialized in his fiction.

No wonder that when Emerson and his friends put together a memorial volume for Fuller it was a volume that arguably diminished her contributions to the world and tried to reduce her to being the kind of woman she sometimes wished she were. Emerson wrote about Margaret with sweetness and distance. Not Hawthorne; he was still distressed. On the subject of Margaret's connections to the man who may or may not have been her husband, Hawthorne responded with rage. Writing eight years after her death, in a fury of his own, Hawthorne lashed out at the woman who had been his friend and muse, and as Elizabeth Hardwick has pointed out, the mud stuck. "She was a great humbug," he wrote, ". . . but she had stuck herself full of borrowed qualities which she chose to provide herself with but which had no root in her. . . . It was such an awful joke, that she should have resolved—in all sincerity no doubt, to be the greatest, wisest, best woman of the age."

Hawthorne, who had been an enigmatic but pleasant member of the communities he inhabited, seemed to change with his success and Margaret's death. "He thinks a good deal of coming to Concord, and possibly to buy a place. Such a plan I would not encourage," wrote Ellery Channing to a friend after a visit to the Hawthornes in the red farmhouse on the Tappan place. He cautioned her to burn the letter after reading it. She didn't. "Assuredly he would get tired of his purchase & then he would be obliged all his days to think of selling or again go to work moving. He always I believe finds fault with the people among whom he settles not at the best a good beginning to make." Struck by the unattractiveness of Sophia and the bad behavior of the Hawthorne children (Una, eight; Julian, six; and Rose, one and a half), Channing had nothing good to say about the family or about the man at its head. Was he right?

The Hawthornes had left the Old Manse in a hurry, chased out by their landlord, the Ripley family, and Emerson's anger. They had all but been run out of Salem after the publication of *The Scarlet Letter.* Now in the Berkshires, they had gotten into a fight with the Tappans—their landlords—over whether or not they were entitled to the apples in the orchard that surrounded their little house.

Caroline Tappan had sharply questioned the Hawthornes' maid as she carried a basket of apples across the orchard to the red shanty. Hawthorne was furious. After all, he and his family were paying rent. Using a kind of verbal savagery only he could muster, he dashed off a letter to the Tappans who, after all, lived in sight of the farmhouse windows and could easily have been visited instead. "I infinitely prefer a small right to a great favor," Hawthorne huffed. "Last year no question of this nature was raised. . . . if you claimed or exercised any manorial privileges it never came to my knowledge."

Caroline Tappan was equally furious about the apples, the presumption of her tenants, and Hawthorne's arrogance. The disagreement colored everyone's feelings. Once friends, they became enemies. It wasn't just the uppity Tappans. Suddenly, the Hawthornes realized that they hated the Berkshires, that the lake had been feeding Hawthorne's allergies, that it was bad for the children, and that the Tappans charged an exorbitant rent for a house in bad repair. They missed eastern Massachusetts with its proximity to Boston. How could they ever have thought they could live so far from the sea?

They were no longer in the position of having to be humiliated by sadistic landlords who looked on them as a charity case. Hawthorne was a famous writer now. By November, they had piled their trunks and belongings into an old farm wagon and set off in a falling snow for the Pittsfield railroad station on their way to West Newton. Sophia's sister Mary had married Horace Mann, and while the Manns were in Washington so that Mann could serve as a congressman, Mary had offered their empty West Newton house to her sister's family.

From West Newton, Hawthorne immediately began looking for a new house, a house commensurate with his standing in the literary community. He found it in the Alcotts' Hillside, abandoned by them for Boston and now empty and for sale. Hawthorne bought the house for $1,500, and a few months later an additional 13 acres for $313. By the spring of 1852, the Hawthornes had moved again, this time coming home to Concord. "Though he actually occupied the place no long time, he had made it his property, and it was more his own home than any of his numerous provisional abodes," wrote Henry James of Hawthorne's final move back to Concord. Hawthorne also said that at the Wayside—he immediately renamed the house—he felt at home for the first time in his life.

"Before Mr. Alcott took it in hand it was a mean-looking affair, with two peaked gables; no suggestiveness about it, and no venerableness although from the style of its construction it seemed to have survived beyond its first century," Hawthorne wrote to his friend George William Curtis. "He added a porch in front and a central peak, and a piazza at each end . . . and invested the whole with a modest picturesqueness." Although Sophia Hawthorne said that the house looked as if it had been inhabited by cattle, no one mentioned the fact that it had once been Horatio Cogswell's pig farm. Just before moving, at the end of May, Hawthorne finished the novel he had written in Lenox, the novel that would become *The Blithedale Romance,* and sent it off to James Fields in Boston.

Although the Hawthornes were happy to be returning to their beloved Concord, a visitor that year, the English writer Arthur Hugh Clough, who had come to Boston with Thackeray and made the pilgrimage out to Concord to visit Emerson, saw it more clearly. "Walk with Emerson to a wood with a prettyish pool," he wrote in his diary of the great, mystical Walden Pond. "Concord is very bare; it is a small sort of village, almost entirely of wood houses, painted white, with Venetian blinds, green outside with two white wooden churches."

It was in planting and landscaping that Bronson Alcott had truly improved the Cogswell property when his family owned it. He had put in grapevines that prettily draped the porches and tiny flower gardens with improvised summerhouses around the property. Behind the house, he had dug the land into a series of terraces traveling up the hill to the ridge where blossoming locust trees, elms, and oaks provided a shady shelter. Here, Hawthorne, literally above it all, would spend many afternoons reading or making notes or just dreaming away the hours. "From the hilltop there is a good view. . . . I know nothing of the history of the house except Thoreau's telling me that it was inhabited, a century or two ago, by a man who believed he should never die."

Sophia was delighted by the new house. She hung the family portrait of Endymion and set up a pedestal for the bust of Apollo. Julian immediately ran over to the Emersons' to play and for a ride on Edward Emerson's pony. Una visited the other Emerson children, and Sophia started giving instruction to some of the local children in the main room of the house.

Moving back to Concord after seven years away felt like a homecoming, but Concord had changed and indeed the world had changed. The courthouse had burned down, but in spite of the advent of the railroad, the population was about the same—about 2,000—and the Irish laborers who had built their shacks by the side of Walden Pond had moved on with the tracks. Most Concord residents were white men and women of English stock, and many of them had lived in Concord for generations. The great conveniences that we take for granted these days were just being invented—the sewing machine, the harvester, and soon the telephone and telegraph and the incandescent lightbulb, as well as all the benefits of electricity. Many more people owned pianos, went to college, or traveled to Europe. In April of 1847, Fanny Longfellow had been the first woman to deliver a child with the aid of ether.

39

PRESIDENT FRANK

———◆———

Not long after the Hawthornes moved in, as they reacquainted themselves with their old Concord neighbors and went for picnics in the woods they remembered so well, something happened that would change their lives in many ways. On June 5, 1852, Hawthorne's old friend and Bowdoin classmate Franklin Pierce was nominated for the presidency by the Democratic National Convention, meeting in Baltimore. Hawthorne immediately wrote to Pierce offering his services as a campaign biographer, and by July he was hard at work. His writing was interrupted by the dreadful death of his sister Louisa, who had been on a journey down the Hudson from Saratoga Springs on the steamer *Henry Clay*.

The *Henry Clay* and the steamer *Armenia* got into a race down the river. As the two boats churned the water side by side, passengers cowered and screamed. Opposite Fort Lee, they collided and swerved apart. The *Henry Clay* plowed into the shoreline, causing explosions and a huge fire. Louisa Hathorne jumped into the Hudson and drowned. Hawthorne was devastated, but the campaign biography could not wait, and by the end of August he had finished it and turned it in.

For all the great advances of civilization in the 1850s, a catastrophe was building that would wipe out thoughts of progress, divide the country, kill off a generation of young men, and effectively end the Concord so loved by the Hawthornes, the Alcotts, the Emersons, and Thoreau. The cloud that would become the Civil War had already appeared on the Concord horizon. Most of the Concord intellectuals were passionate abolitionists, but Hawthorne wavered. His loyalty to Franklin Pierce may have made his position foggier, but he certainly favored the Union and keeping it together at all costs. He thought the Constitution a sacred, inflexible code. He abhorred the Fugitive Slave Act, and he didn't approve of slavery—although like most of his contemporaries he believed that African-Americans were inferior to white men, even as women were.

Franklin Pierce, the blue-eyed friend who had married Jane Appleton, the daughter of Bowdoin's president, while they were still students, had experienced a steady rise to power. As a United States senator, he had turned down an offer to run for vice president, but then suddenly as the dark horse candidate he vaulted ahead of the others— including the incumbent Van Buren—and won the presidency. Historians disparage Pierce, a man with an alcohol problem, a severely depressed wife, and a reputation for cowardice on the battlefield gained during the Mexican-American War. His political good luck seemed to be matched by personal bad luck. The Pierces lost all three of their sons—the last, the beloved Benjamin, died before their eyes during a freak railway accident soon after Pierce was elected president.

But Hawthorne had always liked Pierce, and he always would. His connection to the man who became president that winter of 1853 made Hawthorne suddenly popular. At first, he decided he would take nothing from his old friend, but he soon changed his mind. In March of 1853, Pierce offered Hawthorne the post of American consul in Liverpool, and Hawthorne delightedly accepted. He and the family would spend four years in Liverpool as respected Americans. Their financial problems were over. They would then spend a year on the Continent. Hawthorne was also relieved that he wouldn't have to deal with Sophia's querulous father Dr. Peabody, and generously allowed the Peabody family the use of the Wayside while they were gone.

Perhaps he was also relieved to be escaping the increasingly unpleasant atmosphere in the country as controversy over abolition became more and more heated. He would miss the outrage over John Brown and his sons' murder of five proslavery men at Pottawatomie Creek, Kansas, and some of Brown's heroic reception in Concord, whose wealthier abolitionists raised money for his raid on Harper's Ferry.

Most important, Hawthorne hoped to save enough money to insure his own financial future. Not everyone approved. "Better for me, says my genius, to go cranberrying this afternoon . . . in Gowing's Swamp, to get but a pocketful and learn its peculiar flavor . . . than to go consul to Liverpool and get I don't know how many thousand dollars for it," Thoreau wrote in his journal. But Thoreau didn't have a family to support, or a house to keep up. Hawthorne chose the life; Thoreau chose the work. Thoreau was so pure that, as Hawthorne wrote, "in his presence one feels ashamed of having any money, or a house to live in, or so much as two coats to wear." Thoreau had a point though.

The Hawthornes sailed for England on the *Niagara* and anchored in the Mersey River on July 17. They were now the well-to-do family of a famous writer, complete with a traveling entourage of two maids, who would act as ambassadors for their close friend the American president. It was a very different trip from their last one, the flight from Lenox with all their possessions piled on a cart after the fight over apples with the Tappans. Even as utter despair seemed to inspire the brilliant outpouring of *The Scarlet Letter,* prosperity and daily concerns seemed to undermine Hawthorne's genius. He wouldn't write again for seven years.

The Hawthornes settled in Liverpool, their little family finally safe. When Franklin Pierce lost to Buchanan in 1856, Hawthorne was once again surprised by the vagaries of politics. How could they fire him? They did. Ousted from his job, Hawthorne and his family traveled to London and Paris, and, as they had long planned, decided to spend a year in Rome. But where Margaret Fuller had blossomed and become a happy woman, the Hawthornes struggled and failed. Rome was cold and rainy. Their apartment was dank and the ceilings were so high that it hardly seemed as if they offered any shelter from the out-of-doors.

Hawthorne had grown up and lived in small rooms heated by fires and woodstoves, with low ceilings under practical peaked roofs. In New England, thrift and practicality were necessary and prized. In Rome, people seemed happy to leave their houses in ruins or to let vines grow around the foundations of their huge buildings. There were ruins everywhere, a giant foot at the end of one street, a half-tilted column in a vacant lot, the skeleton of some ancient forum across the piazza. How could they be so oblivious? The Roman way of life, the vast spaces and endless corridors, and the doors so large that smaller doors were cut in them for the use of people, the great courtyards and endless ruins, were unfamiliar.

Hawthorne and his family were also shocked by the nudity in Roman statues and paintings. In nineteenth-century New England, Puritanism still often forbade the mention of female anatomy. Women's clothes were hung on the line to dry draped in sheets and pillowcases lest a male eye fall on them and be led astray by thoughts of nudity. Piano legs were never mentioned, and even chairs often had their legs encased in skirts. In Rome, busts and genitals were everywhere displayed; in public spaces and even in holy places, there were seductive women half-draped and young men with their sex exposed. For a couple from a culture where men and women rarely saw each other naked, the Roman candor was horrifying.

After a miserable winter, the Hawthornes decamped to Florence, where the expatriate colony welcomed them and they became friends— as Margaret had—with Robert Browning and his invalid wife. In Florence, they rented a villa above the city, and they began to like Italy after all. Returning to Rome in the fall felt like a homecoming. If their first winter in Rome had been ruined by culture shock, their second winter was marred by personal tragedy. Their daughter Una, after spending an evening in the Coliseum drawing, came down with a Roman fever that at first seemed mild but which soon became life-threatening. Moaning in pain, pale and feverish, Una endured the worst medications the Roman doctor could think up. It's a miracle that anyone in the nineteenth century survived medical treatment.

Franklin Pierce may not have been a good president, but he was a good friend. Arriving in Rome, he announced that he would not leave until Una was better. A man who had lost his own children, he visited every day and took Hawthorne out for endless walks. They went down the Corso, then past the perpetually windy Piazza del Gesu, where Hawthorne told Pierce a joke he had heard about the wind and the devil. They climbed up the mossy hills past the House of the Vestal Virgins to the top of the Roman Forum and rambled up the Capitoline Hill to peer over the steep edge of the Tarpeian Rock. They walked to St. Peter's great piazza, crossing and recrossing the Tiber. They wandered over to the Piazza Navona and chuckled at the way Bernini in his Fountain of the Four Rivers had made one of the personified rivers appear to be anticipating the collapse of the adjacent Church of St. Agnes, designed by Bernini's rival, Borromini.

Hawthorne began to see Rome as the background of a novel, a novel about a woman with a dreadful secret in her past who unconsciously enlisted a natural man to help her. As he walked the narrow streets near the Palatine Hill, he imagined himself into the heart of a woman who walked there with a past she wanted to forget, a woman who had found her own femininity in a city that was the opposite of his New England and hers. Far from home, he imagined a woman like Margaret and a natural man like his friend Thoreau, and he began writing the book he titled *Transformation*. Rome is a sexy place, once you get used to it, and Hawthorne did. Still, he remained a prude in social matters, refusing to communicate with his friend Louisa Landers because of scandal tied to her name.

The seven years the Hawthornes spent in Liverpool, Florence, and Rome and traveling in between gave them just enough sophistication to be disappointed on their homecoming to Massachusetts. Rome seemed drafty, abhorrently sexual, absurdly, wastefully outsized, but Concord looked like a dreary little village in the steaming heat. Their own Wayside seemed little more than a dilapidated outbuilding. Leaving for Liverpool, Hawthorne's handsomeness was crowned by a mane of thick dark brown hair, while Sophia had her reddish brown hair tied back in an elaborate knot. When they got back to Concord, they both had snow white hair.

40

BAYONETS AND BULLETS

———◆———

The man who brought the horror of the Civil War to Concord was Captain John Brown, a Connecticut native who became a kind of abolitionist guerrilla for the antislavery movement. In January 1847, John Brown traveled to Boston to raise money for what he hoped would be a great slave uprising. He needed guns, ammunition, and at least $30,000 in cash. Clean-shaven, with a high forehead and piercing gray eyes, Brown was a convincing supporter of violence in this just cause. His introduction to Concord came through Franklin Sanborn, the handsome teacher who had come to Concord the year he graduated from Harvard to start a school.

Sanborn was already an eccentric at the age of twenty. He had married an older woman, Ariana Walker, on her deathbed and treasured her letters and a lock of her hair for the rest of his life. Boston loved behavior like that. At Harvard, he was elected to Phi Beta Kappa but declined to accept, saying that the society was an "unjustifiable intellectual aristocracy." Not surprisingly, Emerson tapped him for Concord; not surprisingly, John Brown sought him out on a visit to Boston. He let Sanborn know that Brown's ancestors had come over on the *Mayflower* and fought in the Revolutionary War in the 18th Connecticut Regiment. With his stories of frontier life and Kansas justice, Brown hypnotized his young listener.

Soon enough, Brown was staying with Sanborn for a few days and fund-raising in Concord too. When he arrived in Concord in March to speak at the Town Hall, he was preaching to the furiously converted.

With his prophetic manner, vast fecundity—he had twenty children—
and propensity for quoting the Bible, Brown appeared like something
out of the imagination of the concerned Transcendental circle. The
Town Hall was packed. Brown was on fire for the cause of the slaves,
a fire fed by the self-righteousness of the New Englanders and the
increasingly violent racism of the South. Everyone agreed with him,
but few gave any money. Thoreau thought he was so convincing that
he didn't really need help.

Still, at a reception given for him by Theodore Parker, Brown
could barely keep it together among the men and women he saw as
useless intellectual dandies. His clothes were worn and old; he was
more comfortable by a campfire quoting the Old Testament and
inspiring disciples. "New England had not responded adequately to
his call," writes Edward Renehan in his book about Brown's fund-
raising, *The Secret Six*. "He would not let these millionaires salve
their consciences by throwing him a few morsels from the banquet
that was their life."

A few years later, after United States President Franklin Pierce
signed the Kansas-Nebraska Act into law in 1854, Brown and his sons
became active in Kansas. To the despair of abolitionists, the Kansas-
Nebraska Act replaced the Missouri Compromise, which barred slavery from new territories. The new act gave the new settlers the right to
vote on whether or not to become a slave state or a free state. In Kansas,
the two sides were made up of Yankee abolitionists who had come to
settle, and Missouri residents who came over the border to the east and
wanted Kansas to be a slave state.

In Kansas, the Civil War began in miniature, as Emerson, Thoreau,
and the Alcotts watched from a thousand miles away. Massachusetts
residents who had settled in Kansas were killed and their homes ran-
sacked. People were shot and scalped.

When the town of Lawrence, Kansas, was sacked and burned in
May of 1856, Brown and his men responded in a way that no one
would ever forget. They were also infuriated by the way Senator
Charles Sumner of Massachusetts, after an address on Kansas delivered on the floor of the United States Senate, had recently been beaten
almost to death by South Carolina Senator Preston Brooks with the
gold head of his own cane. "Something is going to be done now,"

Brown raged. "We must show by actual work that there are two sides to this thing and that they can not go on with impunity."

In John Brown's messianic world, an eye for an eye and a tooth for a tooth was the way to show enemies that they would not be unopposed. There would be no more quailing on the part of the righteous Yankees before the unprincipled rebels. In a nighttime raid along the Pottawatomie Creek, Brown and his men, including two of his sons and a son-in-law, called five proslavery men from their houses and executed them. A band of Missourians under a U.S. marshal tried to capture Brown, but the captain ambushed them instead, causing the whole band to surrender. Brown held them hostage and traded them for prisoners.

In 1857, a Missouri slave, Dred Scott, sued for his freedom, arguing that his residence in free states had made him free. In a decision that reaffirmed the Fugitive Slave Act, the United States Supreme Court ruled that slaves were nothing more than property, and that since they had no rights of citizenship they couldn't even petition the courts as Scott had done. When President Buchanan succeeded President Franklin Pierce, the new president asked Congress to admit Kansas as the sixteenth slave state. They balked, and in August of 1858, Kansas voters rejected the expansion of slavery into their state. John Brown's plans expanded. He would lead a full-scale slave revolt. He would infiltrate the southern states. He had formed a "Secret Six Committee" for fund-raising that included Franklin Sanborn and Thomas Wentworth Higginson. President Buchanan put a price of $250 on Brown's head, and Brown offered a mocking $2.50 reward for the capture of President Buchanan.

I am haunted by what happened in the houses along the Pottawatomie the night of John Brown's raid. On a quiet, spring Kansas night, with the crickets chirping and a breeze stirring the leaves of a few oak trees, Brown and his men struck. First, they went to the Doyle farm and captured James P. Doyle and his two sons, William, 22, and Drury, 20, while his wife, daughter, and younger son looked on. The victims were hurried down the road, where John Brown put his revolver to Doyle's head and fired. There was no going back now. The Brown sons fell on the Doyle boys and hacked them down with knives. At the Allen Wilkinson place, they dragged Wilkinson out while his sick wife and children pleaded with them for mercy. They murdered him. Beyond the trees in the dark the prairie stretched out to the horizon. At James Harris's house, they executed William Sherman. There were the knocks on the door, the men being dragged out, and the screams and pleading of their wives and children. There were the howls of pain and fear, the vomiting, the stench as men were slowly, methodically, and brutally murdered to set an example for others. I imagine the blood, the noise of knife against bone, again and again, the shouts and grunts of the murderers, the awful smells of death, and the final dismembered remnants of the men who had just a little while ago been playing with their children or planning a nightcap. The men may have been innocent and their families were certainly innocent.

When Brown and his men were done, they returned to camp and washed their knives in the water of Pottawatomie Creek. With stolen horses, they made their getaway. For years, Brown's sons claimed that their father had no part in the killings but had left it to his two sons. One of them, John, Jr., was apparently driven mad by what had happened that night. Later, when John Brown had become a martyr, what family he had left changed their story. After the massacre at Pottawatomie Creek, fighting began between the Missouri southerners and the Yankee northerners, and the state earned the name of "Bleeding Kansas."

Soon enough, Brown needed more money. By the next spring, he was back in Concord lecturing again in the Town Hall. This time, his full white beard and wild hair gave him the more graphic look of an Old Testament prophet. This time he was on fire, a fire so palpable his listeners could almost feel heat emanating from him as he spoke. He held up a Bowie knife he had taken from the massacred body of one of the Doyle boys and shackles which had been used to tie up one of his sons when he was imprisoned. He attacked materialism and praised the simplicity and goodness of the slaves. Could anyone sit by while men and women were treated as if they were no more important than possessions? Shouldn't everyone give what they could to this great fight, a fight in which Brown was filled with plans and optimistic projections? He didn't talk about what had happened in Kansas, but he didn't conceal it either.

How could Thoreau, Emerson, and the Alcotts have become such fervent admirers and supporters of this violent murderer? Were they too caught up in their translations of Goethe and Pindar to think about anything that happened on a small river in a place called Kansas? Although Emerson's friends Thomas Wentworth Higginson and Franklin Sanborn were also followers of Brown's, others, like John Murray Forbes, thought his eyes looked a little insane. Leaving Concord, Brown visited his wife and some of his children in the Adirondacks and then headed for Harpers Ferry in Virginia, the town where he planned to start off what he was sure would be a widespread rebellion against the oppression of slavery.

"Thoreau and Emerson took John Brown at the value he set himself," says Robert Penn Warren in his biography of John Brown, *John Brown: The Making of a Martyr.* "They didn't give him money . . . but they gave back to the world his own definition of himself. Emerson possessed a set of ideas which had been given the interesting name of Transcendentalism; he spent his life trying to find something in man or nature which would correspond to the fine ideas and the big word. In John Brown Emerson thought he had found his man. . . . 'He believes in two articles,' Emerson told an audience in Concord, speaking about Brown, 'the Golden Rule and the Declaration of Independence. . . . Better that a whole generation of men, women and children should pass away by a violent death, than that one word of either should be violated in this country.' "

Warren's explanation for the guilelessness of the Concord men and women who supported Brown is that they couldn't know who Brown really was. Nevertheless, they gave him the benefit of their own thinking about his mission. Emerson cared about words and lived for their precise meanings; Brown used words only as tools to further his ugly crusade. "And it is only natural that Emerson in his extraordinary innocence, should have understood nothing, nothing in the world, about a man like John Brown to whom vocabulary was simply a very valuable instrument," Warren concludes.

41

LOCAL MARTYR

———◆———

At midnight of Sunday, October 16, 1859, Brown and his men took over the United States Armory in Harpers Ferry, Virginia (in what is now West Virginia). His rebellion didn't last long. President Buchanan ordered in troops, including U.S. Marines under the command of Colonel Robert E. Lee. On Tuesday, Lee asked Brown to surrender; he said he would surrender only if his men could leave the armory unharmed. The troops went in, captured Brown and wounded him, and killed two of his sons. Brown and his few remaining men were taken to the Jefferson County Jail in Charlestown to wait for execution.

Searching the Maryland farmhouse where Brown had gathered his forces for the raid, the federal authorities had come upon some letters implicating northerners who had helped Brown, including the Concord schoolmaster Franklin Sanborn. Sanborn, who ran the successor to the Thoreau brothers' Concord Academy, was ordered to Washington to appear before Congress. He decided not to go. When it was clear that Sanborn was not planning to obey the Senate's request, the Senate's sergeant-at-arms, Dunning R. McNair, dispatched Deputy U.S. Marshal Silas Carleton to arrest him.

On a Tuesday evening in April of 1860, Sanborn answered a knock on his door in the house he also used as a schoolhouse on the Sudbury Road and was met by Carleton, accompanied by three other men with handcuffs. He cried out to his sister, who whipped the horses left by the men out front and roused the neighbors with her screams as the deputies dragged the resisting Sanborn toward the carriage. Church bells started ringing and people poured out of their houses. Sanborn braced himself against the side of the carriage and struggled as the men tried to force him inside. Emerson rushed out of his house, and an attorney found neighbor Judge Hoar, who quickly served a writ of habeas corpus on the intruders. Stones were thrown at the carriage as the deputies unlocked Sanborn and fled for their lives.

If Hawthorne hoped to avoid the whole messy business of the arguments that preceded the Civil War, he would find that impossible. In fact, Sophia Hawthorne's sister Mary Mann, who, after the death of her husband Horace Mann, was living in the Wayside while the Hawthornes were away, was one of the people who hid the fugitive Frank Sanborn in a small upstairs room before he escaped to Canada.

Brown was hung on December 2. The bells of Concord rang in mourning. "The execution of St. John the Just took place on the second," Louisa May Alcott wrote in her diary. "A meeting at the hall, and all Concord was there. Emerson, Thoreau, Father and Sanborn spoke, and all were full of reverence and admiration for the martyr." Many of the Concord men and women had been beside themselves as the date of the execution approached. Somehow, Brown seemed above it all to them, a kind of secular saint who was absolved of his murderous actions by the rightness of his convictions. Alcott, who thought it was criminal to eat a piece of fish because of the agony of the fish, or to take milk from a cow without its permission, or to use an ox to plow a field, went into a kind of mourning for a man who had heartlessly ordered others to be hacked to pieces, and planned a violent rebellion in which his own sons had been killed. "Think much of Capt Brown," Alcott wrote, "this is too noble a man to be sacrificed so; and yet such as he and only such, are worthy of the glories of the cross." Thoreau, the man who couldn't bear to eat flesh and who took his comfort from the animals of the field, the birds and insects, and the great natural world, also compared John Brown to Jesus Christ.

In Thoreau's journals for the winter of 1860, principally studded with charts of the growth of trees and recording of the visits of finches, between a sweet dissertation on hickory trees and white acorns, and a vision of crows on the swamp white oaks over the road beyond Wood's Bridge, comes an argument with his neighbors about Brown. "When I said that I thought he was right, they agreed in asserting that he did wrong because he threw his life away, and that no man had a right to undertake anything which he knew would cost him his life. I inquired if Christ did not foresee that he would be crucified, if he preached such doctrines as he did, but they both, though as if it was their only escape, asserted that they did not believe that he did."

Emerson and Thoreau believed in Brown's mission, and when Francis Merriam, one of Brown's men who had escaped from Harpers Ferry and been put on a train north by Brown's son Owen, made it to Concord in a frightened and disoriented state, Thoreau hitched Emerson's horse Dolly to a carriage and took him to the South Acton Station and put him on a train for Canada. At one point during the journey, Merriam was so disturbed that he tried to escape from the carriage; Thoreau literally had to wrestle him to freedom.

Brown's failed raid on Harpers Ferry and his execution had as large an impact on the political climate of the country as he could have hoped. Between December of 1859 when he was hung, and the firing on Fort Sumter that started the Civil War in April of 1861, the fear of slave uprising and slave revolts was in the forefront of many white minds. When there were slave uprisings, usually quelled with a huge loss of life among those who revolted, they were called repeats of Harpers Ferry; John Brown was often referred to.

The right-thinking men and women of Concord seem to have been overwhelmed by a sense of their own rightness. Slavery was evil, so everything that opposed slavery had to be good. For the moment, the slavery issue and the horrors it had engendered were also very far away. Perhaps Thoreau and Alcott were still immature boys who had never been able to support themselves, dazzled by Brown's bravery and brilliance. They were easy to fool for a passionate con artist in desperate need of money for his chosen cause. But even Emerson, the imminently practical father figure for those feckless boys, went along.

In a speech he gave in Boston in November while Brown awaited execution, he called Brown "that new saint than whom none purer or more brave was ever led by love of men into conflict and death—the new saint awaiting his martyrdom, who . . . will make the gallows glorious like the cross."

In Cambridge, men seemed calmer. Emerson's friend Henry Wadsworth Longfellow noted December 2 in his diary: "This will be a great day in our history; the date of a new Revolution—quite as much needed as the old one. Even now as I write they are leading old John Brown to execution in Virginia for attempting to rescue slaves! This is sowing the wind to reap the whirlwind, which will come soon." Longfellow, less besotted with Brown than his neighbors, had it right. The Civil War, when it came, would destroy Concord and decimate New England. By the time it was over, both Hawthorne and Thoreau would be dead, Emerson would be on the path to the severe Alzheimer's disease that crippled him so completely that at the end of his life he couldn't spell Concord, and Louisa May Alcott would have changed from a dreaming girl into an angry, sick, and very practical middle-aged spinster.

Were they the victims of a greedy, warmongering South? Or did they help bring on the catastrophe with their own willful innocence and self-righteousness? "Most of the people who sat about him in those parlors," Warren writes of Brown's last fund-raising tour of New England, "and gave him their earnest attention, found something peculiarly congenial to their own prejudices and beliefs. Captain Brown was a 'higher law man.' He was 'superior to any legal tradition'—just as most of these people felt themselves to be—and if he claimed to have a divine commission, they could understand what he meant. . . . Unhappily, a corollary of this divine revelation was to make the South pay, and pay again. The disagreement might conceivably have been settled under terms of law, but when it was transposed into terms of theology there was no hope of settlement. There is only one way to conclude a theological argument: bayonets and bullets."

The Transcendentalists, as Warren acidly notes, were thinkers who did take everything personally and who saw theology in birdsongs and rainstorms. Emerson after all had been drummed out of his church for refusing to take communion because it seemed to him that the bread and wine were not the body and blood after all. He didn't want to deal with symbols anymore. Then he had been drummed out of Harvard for suggesting that God was something that could be found in nature or in other people as well as in the gorgeous confines of religion. God, in other words, was a personal matter.

In his one hundredth lecture at the Concord Lyceum in 1880, a lecture patched together by his daughter and his secretary because he was too far gone to write his own lectures and almost too far gone to deliver them, Emerson tried to define what had happened in the group of people he had so forcefully brought together in Concord. "I think there prevailed . . . a general belief . . . that there was some concert of *doctrinaires* to establish certain opinions and inaugurate some movement . . . of which design the supposed conspirators were quite innocent," the old man, now seventy-seven and one of the last living vestiges of the Concord community, told his eager audience; "there was no concert, and only here and there two or three men or women who read and wrote, each alone with unusual vivacity. Perhaps they only agreed in having fallen upon Coleridge and Wordsworth and Goethe, then on Carlyle, with pleasure and sympathy. . . . I suppose all of them were surprised at this rumor of a school or sect, and certainly at the name Transcendentalism, given nobody knows by whom, or when it was first applied. . . . From that time meetings were held for conversation with very little form, from house to house, of people engaged in studies, fond of books, and watchful of all the intellectual light from whatever quarter it flowed. . . . Nothing more serious came of it than the modest quarterly journal called *The Dial*. . . . all its papers were unpaid contributions . . . . perhaps its writers were its chief readers."

As the old man spoke, leaning against the wooden lectern, some listeners' eyes wandered to the building's high arched windows, to the traces of green just visible on the great elms outside, to the buds on the lilac bushes bunched around the Middlesex Hotel across the street. Under the deep tones of the old man's voice, they heard the sound of the finches on the grass near the Civil War monument to the men Concord had lost, and the faraway splash of the river under the Milldam and the soft swish of the Concord River flowing fast through the abutments of the Old North Bridge. It had been more than a hundred years since revolution had come to Concord, marching down the Lexington Road past the Cogswell farm in the form of a parade of British soldiers in their red coats with muskets at arms.

The intellectual revolution had taken longer, but, paid for by Emerson, and amused by Alcott, it had come as certainly as the glorious days of 1776. It was a revolution that gently toppled God off his throne and replaced him with nature, with the glory of the physical world, and with the best things in the human heart. It freed men and women from the slavery of Calvinism. It blossomed in Thoreau's ideas and in his beautiful portrait of nature and in Hawthorne's brilliantly etched portraits of society, and finally with a Louisa May Alcott novel that memorialized the whole fabulous time.

Part Four

42

THE DEATH OF THOREAU

———◆———

As the Civil War approached and the residents of Concord were interrupted by the sounds of Massachusetts troops drilling in the street or being seen off at the railroad station, both Thoreau and Hawthorne began to die. At the strawberry party that Emerson threw on the day after the Hawthornes returned from Europe, Hawthorne, Emerson, Thoreau, and Louisa May Alcott all chatted and celebrated their beloved Concord. Edward Emerson gave the other children rides on his pony. They were all home again.

Thoreau first got sick in 1855, soon after the publication of *Walden*. He had had some bouts with tuberculosis, and the function of his lungs had been critically weakened by his working with lead and fine, fine sawdust in close quarters at the family pencil factory. It was almost as if the great effort of writing and revising *Walden* had drained him entirely. Then his father's death in 1859 was another unexpected blow. What was left of Thoreau sometimes seemed unbearably unfocused. His gnomic side had overtaken his fierce, organized rationality. He and Emerson made up, resumed their old friendship, and started going for their walks together, but Emerson was sometimes unsure who his friend had become. His pronouncements now seemed more vague than wise.

When Thoreau would make some obscure orphic remark about Emerson being happy to eat moss, Emerson sometimes wished for a saner companion. On the other hand, when he compared Thoreau to the politicians and bankers he met in Boston society, and whom he hated for their materialism and pompous self-congratulation, he was happy to spend time with his old friend.

Thoreau got better and then worse again, and by the early spring of 1862 he had returned to the family house he had helped build on Texas Street—now named Thoreau Street. At first, he stayed upstairs in his little attic room lined with his books. There Louisa May Alcott, herself very sick, visited him. Finally, as he got sicker and began to get even thinner than he had always been, he was moved downstairs, where a bed had been made up for him that would be more convenient for the stream of visitors who came to pay homage. At last, after years of uncomfortable coexistence, Concord loved Thoreau. All his unconventional ways had been forgotten. The fire, the night in jail, the bad table manners, the scruffy looks, seemed less important than his endurance and sweetness. He advised young Edward Emerson to carry an arrowhead in his pocket and told his sister that he had always loved Ellen Sewall. When one minister asked him what he saw in the future as he stood so near the brink, he said with a flash of his old wit, "One world at a time."

When another visitor to his bedside asked if he had made his peace with God, Thoreau shot back, "I didn't know we had ever quarreled." He died at nine in the morning on May 6, and on May 9 the village schools were dismissed so that the children he had so loved could go to his funeral; Louisa May Alcott went with her father and sister to church as the bells tolled forty-four times, once for each year of Thoreau's life.

The coffin was covered with wildflowers, and the services were held in the First Baptist Church. Bronson Alcott read a few passages from Thoreau's writing. It was a beautiful spring afternoon; the lilacs were just budding in the dooryard of the Colonial Inn, the new hotel on Monument Square. Green leaves had begun to paint the great trees around the cemetery and along the roads, and the wood thrush and phoebe called out as if to welcome the man who understood their song as the procession, which included the dignitaries of Concord and the schoolchildren of Concord, made its way across the green to the New Burying Ground (later renamed Sleepy Hollow Cemetery). Louisa May Alcott, still shaken and wearing a cap, made the sad walk to the cemetery. Hawthorne and Sophia stood at the grave with the crowd of mourners. Emerson read a eulogy, an essay on his friend that would be his last major piece of writing. Emerson would always remember Thoreau as his best friend, even later when his memory loss became so acute that he couldn't remember his best friend's name.

Now, at the lectern of the church, he brought Thoreau back to life for his listeners. Starting with the facts, Emerson slowly warmed up to one of the most extraordinary essays ever written by one friend about another. The essay captures Thoreau's high principles and his sense of humor, his stubbornness and his accuracy. "No truer American existed than Thoreau," Emerson said. "He lived for the day, not cumbered and mortified by his memory. If he brought you yesterday a new proposition, he would bring you today another not less revolutionary." Then after quoting a dozen aphorisms from Thoreau's unpublished manuscripts, he ended with an accurate prophecy. "The country knows not yet, or in the least part, how great a son it has lost. It seems an injury that he should leave in the midst his broken task which no one else can finish, a kind of indignity to so noble a soul that he should depart out of nature before yet he has been really shown to his peers for what he is. But he, at least, is content. His soul was made for the noblest society; he had in a short life exhausted the capabilities of this world. Wherever there is knowledge, wherever there is virtue, wherever there is beauty, he will find a home."

43

LOUISA IN
WASHINGTON, D.C.

———◆———

Now approaching middle age, Louisa was painfully restless. "Had a funny lover who met me in the cars, said he lost his heart at once," she confided in her journal in 1860. "Handsome man of forty. A southerner, and very demonstrative and gushing, called and wished to pay his addresses, and being told I didn't wish to see him, retired, to write letters and haunt the road with his hat off, while the girls laughed and had great fun. He went at last, and peace reigned. My adorers are all queer."

Louisa's potboilers were bringing in some money, but she had begun thinking about a great novel, a long, more serious work that would memorialize Thoreau and pin some of her most delicious childhood memories to the page forever. It would begin with a young girl taking a wonderful river trip with two men. It would be about the confusions of love and the men—idealized versions of Thoreau and Emerson—who had the most impact on her life with their generosity and intelligence. She wasn't ready to start writing, but she couldn't sit still.

In November just before her family and the neighbors celebrated her thirtieth birthday, which marked the official beginning of her spinsterhood, Louisa decided the time had come for her to do something about freeing the slaves. Dorothea Dix had been appointed the country's first supervisor of nursing. Until the Civil War, most nurses had been men; women who worked with wounded men were thought to be little more than prostitutes or camp followers. Dix set out to change that with a call for women of impeccable moral character between the ages of thirty-five and fifty. Dix, who was called Dragon Dix by the women who worked for her because of the discipline she maintained with her corps of women, wanted women who were strong, matronly, sober, neat, and industrious. Just before her birthday, Louisa decided to apply for work as a nurse in Washington, D.C., under Dorothea Dix; her experience was limited to her own nursing of her dying sister and a close reading of Florence Nightingale. Her orders from Miss Dix came through in December. At last, she was off on the train to New London, the boat to New York, and a second train from Jersey City to Washington.

The trip south was exciting and scary. She lost her tickets and found her tickets and lost them again. A coupling iron on the train broke and had to be repaired. "The country through which we passed did not seem so very unlike that which I had left, except that it was more level and less wintry," wrote Louisa in the transparent prose in which all her writing self-consciousness fell away. "In summer time the wide fields would have shown me new sights, and the way-side hedges blossomed with new flowers; now everything was sere and sodden, and a general air of shiftlessness prevailed. . . . Dreary little houses with chimneys built outside, with clay and rough sticks piled crosswise, as we used to build cob towers, stood in barren looking fields, with a cow pig or mule lounging about the door." Without knowing it, in her journals of the trip, Louisa had already hit upon the mature style that would leave the mannered melodrama of the past behind.

Arriving in Washington thrilled and confused her. "The White House was lighted up, and carriages were rolling in and out of the great gate. . . . Pennsylvania Avenue with its bustle, lights, music and military, made me feel as if I'd crossed the water and landed somewhere in Carnival time." The carnival was soon over. Louisa was a woman used to discomfort, and so at first the routine at the grim building that had been made over into the Union Hotel Hospital, the curtainless room with its narrow beds, the cold-water bathing, and the awful food—bread and butter and a rasher of bacon washed down with a pint of coffee—was easily overcome. The Alcotts were vegetarians, but she ate the fried army beef without complaint. As she had traveled south to Washington, the Union Army led by the handsome West Point General Ambrose Everett Burnside (his fancy whiskers gave the English language the term sideburns) was cooling its heels on the banks of the Rappahannock River in Virginia about twenty miles south of the city. Washington itself was a half-built capital—the Washington Monument had been abandoned and the bottom half of its plinth jaggedly marked the sky near the unfinished dome of the Capitol. Burnside's dallying allowed Confederate Generals Stonewall Jackson and James Longstreet to mass their troops and dig in on the hillsides above the river.

On December 13, just as Louisa was settling in at the hospital, Burnside ordered his charge, which was repelled by the Confederates. Undaunted by the pointless slaughtering of his men, General Burnside ordered charge after charge—fourteen in all. Almost 13,000 men were killed; Fredericksburg was to be one of the worst defeats in the history of the United States Army. At dawn the next day, everyone in the old Union Hotel heard a thundering knock as the first casualties began to arrive. Looking out the grimy window, Louisa saw forty wagons that looked like market carts lined up in the street. Each cart was overflowing with wounded, dead, whimpering, screaming soldiers. Men with missing limbs, bandaged heads blackened with powder, men howling in pain. She watched them suffer, and half the time she watched them die. The smell of rotting flesh, blood, and dirt overwhelmed the damp medicinal smells of the hospital.

With her three days' experience as a nurse, Louisa started washing the wounded, stroking and sudsing half-naked male bodies. She had never seen a naked male body. She was terrified, but she kept that to herself. She carried a bottle of lavender water to ward off the bad smells that overwhelmed the hospital, but it wasn't much use. Soon she was promoted to being the night nurse. She sat with the wounded at night as they started awake screaming.

She followed Dr. George Winfield Stipp, the hospital's surgeon in charge, from ward to ward and watched him do amputations and sutures. She comforted the survivors of the surgeries. On her new shift from midnight until noon, she worked harder than she had ever worked. No sleep. Awful food. She sleepwalked through Christmas, and suddenly a flash of an imagined Christmas in Concord with her happy family gathered around the tree gave her a jolt. Then back to the wounded and dying. By January, Louisa felt awful. A spell of coughing would hit her and she had to lay down whatever she was carrying, and stop whatever she was doing until it passed. The smell of gangrene and oils and death seemed overwhelming.

Dr. Stipp said she had pneumonia, or perhaps typhoid. On the theory that the less material there was in the body, the less progress a disease could make, medical practice in the 1860s involved the ingestion of laxatives like cassia, castor oil, and magnesium in large quantities, followed by powerful cathartics like calomel. The body must be emptied so that the disease would not be able to take root. Calomel, a mercury compound, was given for almost everything—fever, pneumonia, hepatitis, and laryngitis—and given in huge doses. Accepted practice was to dose with calomel until the point of salivation—a sign of acute mercury poisoning. The tongue became swollen, the gums excruciatingly painful, and the hair fell out. The long-term effects on the nervous system were even more severe—weakness, stiffness of joints, delirium, and restlessness.

With the best medicine he knew how to practice, Dr. Stipp slowly poisoned Louisa's nervous system, as Sophia Peabody's nervous system had been poisoned by her own father. Louisa sustained doses that would make her an invalid long after the pneumonia had passed. Like Sophia before her, Louisa was a victim of medicine, not of disease. She got sicker. She kept working, but finally Miss Dix intervened and told her that she had to stop. The Union Army was losing, at Bull Run and at Shiloh, where 23,000 men were killed. The *Monitor* and the *Merrimack* fought, and the days of the wooden ships were over. Only six weeks after Louisa had left for Washington, hoping at last to have a benevolent effect in the world, her father took the boat and the train down to get her and bring her, a wasted and sick ghost of a woman, home to her own bedroom in Orchard House.

Looking back at nineteenth-century medicine, when doctors often made patients fatally ill with their cures for diseases they could barely define, it seems a world away from the miracles of modern medicine, medicine that can save the life of a premature baby or give useful and happy decades to men struck down by heart disease. Still, there are some parallels. My uncle who is a doctor taught me the word "iatrogenic," which means "caused by the doctor," and he said that it often crops up in medical practice. Our lives are rich with examples—hormone replacement therapy, for instance—of medicines that may hurt a patient more than they help. Still, when doctors hurt patients these days, they don't automatically prescribe morphine for the pain as the nineteenth-century doctors did. Like her friend Sophia, Louisa May Alcott developed an addiction to morphine and opium that she never lost.

44

RETURN AND ILLNESS

———◆———

At home, Dr. Bartlett diagnosed Louisa with typhoid; that disease, he said, explained the shivering and chills, which actually came from mercury poisoning. Her hair was shaved, what was left of it, and she lay in bed too sick to care. A fever turned her face deep red, and the coughing fits racked her shivering body. She could not forget the men, boys really, the wounded and dying, the screaming and sobbing. John Suhre, the Virginia blacksmith whose lungs had been ripped open by a Confederate ball, and Patrick Murray, who might never walk again, and Sergeant Bane, who was learning to write with his left hand, and Richard Fitzgerald with his wounded arm, and the stories they told her in the long nights as the darkness outside slowly turned to grey and then finally into dawn.

Louisa was the one in her family and in the Concord community who had never been sick. She had helped with Lidian Emerson and with Thoreau, with her own sister and with Una Hawthorne, and now the community turned out to help her. The Hawthornes insisted that Louisa's mother eat with them to save her the trouble of cooking, the Emersons sent over a maid to help. Orchard House became a hospital as Louisa raved upstairs. Dreadful images floated in front of her of evil men and wounded men in need, of the battlefront and kidnappings. Her body wasted away, her hands stiffened with inflammatory rheumatism, and she was unable to sleep. Her mouth was covered with sores. Her gums throbbed with pain, and her legs were too weak for her to leave her bed. The pain in her back was excruciating, and Dr. Bartlett started giving her larger doses of opium.

Mrs. Bliss, a woman who said she had "special healing powers" and who had worked for Horace Greeley, came to Orchard House one afternoon in February. Holding Louisa's hands, she worked to "magnetize" the pain out of her. First there was an easing of the back torture, then almost miraculously Louisa was able to stand, and slowly she got better—or as much better as she would ever get. Her hair was gone, although it would eventually grow back sparsely, a sad replacement for her yard of chestnut silk. She began wearing caps over her bald head and started relearning the arts of walking, sitting, and eating. She started learning to write with her left hand, as her right was too cramped to be useful.

The three-month crisis seemed to be the death of the old Louisa, the hoping, dreaming girl with the long glossy hair. The combination of the sights and sounds of war seen up close and her devastating illness had pulled away whatever was left of her as a young woman and left a refined intelligence ready for action. As her womanly self receded, she began to find a professional energy and success that had eluded her in the painful years of struggle before she turned thirty. Missing her friend Thoreau in the long hospital nights, devastated by his death, she had written a poem for him that fell out of her papers when she got home. Her father read it and passed it on to the Hawthornes, who in turn passed it on to James Fields, the very ogre who had told Louisa that she couldn't write. Fields had changed his mind. Almost effortlessly, it seemed, her poem was published in the *Atlantic Monthly.*

> *Spring came to us in guise forlorn;*
> *The bluebird chants a requiem;*
> *The willow-blossom waits for him;—*
> *The Genius of the wood is gone.*

The letters she had written to her family from the Union Hotel Hospital, reshaped and reordered and titled *Hospital Sketches,* were published in *Commonweal,* a new magazine run by the returned Franklin Sanborn. The issue sold out. *Sketches* were reprinted and quoted everywhere; suddenly Louisa May Alcott was an established writer. In the meantime, her potboilers like "Pauline's Passion and Punishment," written for *Frank Leslie's Illustrated Newspaper* under the pseudonym A. M. Barnard, were also bringing in hundreds of dollars. In the year 1863, Louisa made $600 from her writing, and she began thinking again about tackling a serious novel.

Louisa began to live in the head of a young girl like herself named Sylvia Yule who falls passionately in love with her brother's friend Adam. "A massive head covered with rings of ruddy brown hair, gray eyes that seemed to pierce through all disguises . . . power, intellect, and courage were stamped on his face and figure, making him the manliest man that Sylvia had ever seen." Adam, a "masterful soul, bent on living out his beliefs and aspirations at any costs," is Thoreau. But in fiction as in life, the stubborn, dark-haired young girl meets a million obstacles to her great love. The book began to possess Louisa's imagination. "Genius burned so fiercely that for four weeks I wrote all day and planned nearly all night," she wrote. "I was perfectly happy and seemed to have no wants."

With its creaky plot and contrived narration, *Moods* was a step backward for Louisa as a writer. The prose is far from the works of A. M. Barnard in content, but not really in style. In the book, Sylvia marries the wrong man, thinking through a misunderstanding that Adam is already spoken for. He's not, of course, and when they both realize what has happened—simultaneously with realizing their love—there is much sadness and questioning. Sylvia then returns to her rightful husband, and both Adam and the husband die in a shipwreck heavily reminiscent of the shipwreck in which Margaret Fuller drowned. In 1864, Louisa gave the book to the publisher Aaron Loring, who took his time asking her to cut it in half. The new Louisa May Alcott didn't hesitate. In intense months of rewriting, she brought it down to under 300 pages, and it was published in 1864.

"I hope success will sweeten me," she wrote in a note to her mother that she enclosed in the first copy of the book, "and make me what I long to become, more than a great writer—a good daughter." *Moods* sold out three editions, although it reached many fewer readers than Louisa had imagined. Worse, it got scathing reviews. Henry James wrote, "The two most striking facts with regard to 'Moods' are the author's ignorance of human nature and her self-confidence in spite of this ignorance." His review appeared in the July 1865 issue of the *North American*. Later, James changed his mind.

Richmond fell on April 3, 1865, but the rejoicing in the Union was short-lived; Lincoln was assassinated two weeks later on April 19. The world outside Louisa's imagination was celebrating the Union victory, mourning Lincoln's assassination, and celebrating all over again. On a visit to her sister Anna's house to help care for her baby boy, a dream of Louisa's came true in the form of an invitation to go to Europe as a companion for Anna Minot Weld. "On the 19th (of July) we sailed in the *China,* Anna and George Weld and myself. John, Lucy and Mrs. May went to see me off. I could not realize that my long desired dream was coming true, & fears that I might not see all the dear home faces when I came back made my heart very full as we steamed down the harbor & Boston vanished," Louisa wrote in her journal.

Louisa's time in Europe was another kind of growing up. "Such perfect shades of color, delighted one's eyes, for grass was never so green, wheat so deeply golden, woods so dark or rivers bluer than those," she wrote to her father after traveling by train through the Kent countryside on the way from Paris back to London. "Nothing was abrupt, nobody in a hurry, and nowhere did you see the desperately go-ahead style of life that we have. The very cows in America look fast, and the hens seem to cackle fiercely over their rights like strong minded old ladies, but here the plump cattle stood up to their knees in clover, with a reposeful air that is very soothing, and the fowls cluck contentedly as if their well disciplined minds accepted the inevitable spit with calm resignation, and the very engine instead of a shrill devil-may-care yell, like ours, did its duty in one gruff snort like a beefy giant with a cold in its head."

By the time Louisa boarded one of the last wooden coal eaters to cross the Atlantic, the *Africa,* she had been away for a year and was anxious to be home. On July 19, 1864, Louisa landed in New York, and John Pratt, her sister Anna's husband, was there to meet her. It was thrilling to return to Concord and be welcomed by her parents and sisters, the Emersons, the Hawthornes, Franklin Sanborn, and everyone she had grown up with. But Concord looked different after Rome, Paris, and London. It seemed small and pokey, the houses drafty, and the dirt roads dusty. The downtown looked more like a crossroads than a city, with its loafers out on the Milldam doing nothing as the world passed by, and its few pathetic shops. Her parents were in dire shape. Her mother's health was deteriorating and the family debts mounting and unattended to. Anna was living at home in Orchard House with her boys because her husband couldn't support them all. Age had taken its toll. Anna had an ear trumpet and saw John only on weekends, Abba's eyes were failing and the house needed repairs.

Louisa set to work with a will and began churning out stories for magazines and thrillers for Thomas Niles, who had become her editor. Potboilers like *Behind a Mask* were what brought in money even in dribs and drabs. With few breaks, she kept on working, running the household, and paying its expenses. Her mother was sliding into senility, and Louisa took care of her and hired a woman to bathe her and give her massages. Bronson couldn't cope. What is it like to have parents who behave like children? Louisa, her own needs unmet and even unacknowledged, was kept busy with her mother's emotional ups and downs and her mother's need for an eye operation in Boston and her father's airy refusal to have anything to do with the adult world.

By Christmas, Louisa herself was sick again; at the age of thirty-five she had been through a lifetime of difficulty. The stress of running the household and caring for her parents and paying for everything seemed to have triggered another bout of mercury poisoning. She had agonizing pains in her legs and arms and often could do no more than sit in a dark room and tremble.

By June, she was better, but Orchard House, inhabited by its two aging parents who acted like children and two sisters who acted like children, was a place that Louisa decided was bad for her writing. She blithely rented an apartment on Hayward Place in Boston and took a job as the editor of *Merry's Museum,* a children's magazine. In a letter to Moses Coit Tyler, a married fan who had been her guide around London and who was a professor at the University of Michigan, she seemed giddy with relief. "I still cherish the dream of returning for another revel in dear, dirty delightful London," she wrote. "Before sailing I'll drop you a line suggesting that you put your University in one pocket, your family in another, & come too." And she invited him to call, if he ever came to Boston, at "Gamp's Garret" on Hayward Place.

Her urban idyll was brief. Thomas Niles had been pressuring her to write a girls' story, and she resisted. She did not want to write for a younger audience. After all her work, she had earned the privilege of writing adult novels. Stymied, Niles was too shrewd to give in. Instead of nagging Louisa, he did the one thing which he knew would work; he appealed to Bronson. "Now I suppose you will come home soon and write your story," Bronson wrote her with the mesmeric power he seemed to have over the women in his family. By May, a reluctant Louisa was back in Concord.

45

HAWTHORNE LEAVES
CONCORD

———◆———

Whenever Hawthorne left home, he got into trouble. His heroes and heroines are all outcasts, people who with all the best intentions have found themselves spurned by their own communities. Community and its intolerance was one of his great themes. It was also one of the themes in his own life and the life of his family.

As a young man, he and his hapless bride Sophia were expelled from Concord. Back in Salem, his political clumsiness made him and his family pariahs. In Lenox, the fight over apples precipitated yet another hurried, angry leave-taking.

Concord, the Hawthornes came to believe, was their true place on earth. The place they could stay. In returning to Concord and buying the Wayside, next to the Alcotts and across the road from Emerson, they imagined they were joining a community that would accommodate their twitches and quirks, their difficult opinions and dark writing. They were coming home. But the merriment of the Emersons' welcoming strawberry party soon wore off, and the thing that always happened began to happen again.

First, on Thoreau's death, Hawthorne began writing about his friend. He started a profile, and a romance as well, called "Septimius Felton." But politics overwhelmed him, as it was overwhelming everyone in Concord and in the whole country. Hawthorne was not good at politics, and once again they got him into trouble. At a time when people in Concord worshiped President Abraham Lincoln, Hawthorne visited Washington and wrote that Lincoln was "about the homeliest man I ever saw." Lincoln was "honest at heart," Hawthorne admitted, but he was also "in some sort sly—at least endowed with a sort of tact and wisdom that are akin to craft." A cool intellect that tended to see both sides of any argument and tended to challenge the conventional wisdom, Hawthorne found himself living among people who could brook no doubts about the cause of abolition or the magnificence of the Union Army.

The situation was made worse by Hawthorne's friendship with former President Franklin Pierce—Hawthorne called him in anagram Princlie Frank. But worst of all was Hawthorne's attitude toward Concord's brand-new saint, the revered John Brown. Unlike Thoreau, Emerson, or the Alcotts, Hawthorne took the trouble to visit Harpers Ferry, but it did not change his mind about Brown, whom he called a "blood-stained fanatic." "Nobody was ever more justly hanged," Hawthorne wrote, putting himself at odds with his neighbors across the street and next door who had worn out their pen nibs comparing Brown to Jesus Christ. Tension built when the Alcotts, just a stone's throw away, took in John Brown's daughters as boarders after the firing on Fort Sumter and the Concord regiment's formation and departure.

Hawthorne didn't even seem to care about the preservation of the Union. "New England will still have her rocks and ice. . . . As to the South I never loved it. We do not belong together, the Union is unnatural, a scheme of man not an ordinance of God," he wrote. Elizabeth Peabody's furious abolitionism came crashing down on the rocks of her sister Sophia's loyalty to her husband. The two sisters were at last able to get down and fight about the man they had been implicitly fighting over for decades.

For all her noble intelligence and her generosity to other writers, Elizabeth's life had not gone well; she had become a kind of cartoon fat aunt for her sister's children. Julian, in a heartbreaking passage in his journals, tells how Aunt Elizabeth once visited and, sitting in the big chair, was disturbed by the family cat's yowling and meowing. The cat seemed to be protesting Aunt Elizabeth's very existence. When Aunt Elizabeth finally stood up, it was revealed that she was sitting on a litter of kittens. They were all dead, slowly smothered as their mother had howled her protest. Now Aunt Elizabeth became Elizabeth the righteous. Sophia fought back as well as she could. "My husband is on dangerous ground," she reminded the sister who had once been that husband's number-one fan. "I cannot let anyone be saucy about him to me." Another twenty-one-page defense rubbed salt in old wounds by asking the spurned Elizabeth, "How can you tell anything about our innermost life of thought? Is it not arrogant to presume to know, still more deny, our yearnings for humanity. Especially how can you know Mr. Hawthorne's sentiments, when he has not communicated with you for twenty years? Why cannot you rest in peace about his sentiments, whatever they may be?"

Even as Hawthorne sank money he didn't have into renovating his family's new home, and as his children entered school and bonded with the Emerson children across the street, Hawthorne got away from it all by traveling up instead of out. He spent more and more time on the private leafy terraces above the Wayside, and arranged to have the endlessly renovating carpenters build him a private tower high above the house and high above the roiling opinions of Concord and his neighbors. At the same time, Hawthorne began to look and feel sicker every day. By the time the *Atlantic Monthly* published his essay "Chiefly About War Matters"—an essay so inflammatory that even his beloved editor James Fields asked him to make some changes in the disagreeable way he described President Lincoln and the agreeable way he described some Confederate soldiers—he felt tired all the time. By January, when a broken, very sick Louisa May Alcott returned to Orchard House from her six weeks in Washington, Hawthorne wasn't sure if he was ill or just depressed and discouraged.

There was constant trouble with the neighbors. Garrulous Bronson Alcott had the habit of sitting under his elm tree on his own rustic bench waiting for travelers on the road. He would offer them an apple and take his payment by subjecting them to endless lectures on education, on the nature of children, on the differences between England and America. No longer doing his "Conversations" as public performances, he did them privately, and Hawthorne wasn't interested. He tried to avoid Alcott, hiding in the sky tower or taking a carriage into town. Bronson was a boor, and his wife was a hysteric whose sensationalism drove Sophia Hawthorne almost as crazy as her husband's pedagogy drove Nathaniel Hawthorne. Complaining to her friend Annie Fields, Sophia wrote in a letter that Mrs. Alcott had announced that the rebels had taken Washington, an announcement that caused Sophia a week of nightmarish anxiety and which turned out to be false. "Mrs. Alcott is the most appalling sensationalist," she wrote. "She frightens me out of my five senses from time to time with telling me one thing and another and suggesting blood-curdling possibilities."

On a January Sunday in 1864, Bronson walked next door to ask if there was a problem. The Hawthornes restricted their complaints to describing Abba as a person "totally devoid of the power to tell the truth." Without apologizing, Bronson acknowledged that his wife was as they described her. The Hawthornes assured Bronson that they would be steadfast neighbors if they were ever needed in an emergency. They carefully avoided the subject of politics.

In spite of smoothing over his neighborly frictions with the Alcotts, things just got worse for Hawthorne. When he had readied his book about living in England for publication, it was titled *Our Old Home;* he sent it along to an eager James Fields with its strong, loving dedication to Franklin Pierce. The dedication made Fields much less eager. Hawthorne refused to withdraw the dedication. "If he is so exceedingly unpopular that his name is enough to sink the column," he wrote to Fields, "there is so much more the need that an old friend should stand by him."

Fields, at an impasse, asked Ellery Channing to talk with Hawthorne about withdrawing the dedication. Channing, not eager for a confrontation, passed the task on to the willing Elizabeth Peabody, who wrote a furious letter to her brother-in-law, a letter that seemed to exhaust Hawthorne rather than enrage him. He was sick of gossip, sick of argument, and sick to death of being told what to think. After pointing out in as many ways as he could that he wasn't going to change his mind, he ended his response to Elizabeth more in sorrow than in anger. "I do not write," he chided her, "(if you will please to observe) for my letter to be read to others. . . . The older I grow the more I hate to write notes, and I trust I have here written nothing that may make it necessary for me to write another."

46

DEATH

———◆———

Although the direction of the Civil War changed in July of 1863 with the decimation of the Confederate Army in Pickett's Charge at Gettysburg—Lee on his side seeming as misled as Burnside had seemed earlier at Fredericksburg—the war between Hawthorne and his neighbors and relatives continued. Hawthorne wouldn't have to write many more notes. By 1864, when General Ulysses S. Grant took control of the Union armies and began sweeping south into Virginia, anyone who visited Hawthorne could see that he didn't care anymore. He was dying. Visitors were kept away. He sat in his bathrobe day after day staring at the fire. After an encounter with Oliver Wendell Holmes on the street in May, Holmes told James T. Fields's wife Annie what he thought. "OWH thinks the shark's tooth is on him," she wrote in her diary, "but would not have this known."

Once again Franklin Pierce came to the rescue. He would whisk Hawthorne away to New Hampshire and give him the benefit of long talks, a sympathetic ear, and fresh mountain air—although New Hampshire in May is not warm. Pierce's wife Jane had died the year before, and perhaps he thought that shared grief would be easier to bear than lonely grief. He and Hawthorne left Concord and arrived in Concord, New Hampshire, a few days later. It was cold and Hawthorne was too sick to continue. By Monday, spring seemed looming, the trees showed traces of leaves and blossoms, and the two men started north again.

The carriage rocked and swayed as they creaked north from Concord, up the Pemigewasset River valley to Center Harbor on the shores of Squam Lake, where loons called out to them and pines marched down to the sandy shore. At the head of the lake in the town of Plymouth, they checked into the Pemigewasset House across from the railroad station. They had talked about the beauties of a peaceful death, and now as Pierce made plans to stay in Plymouth for a while and ask Sophia to join them, Hawthorne had a simple dinner of tea and toast and went to bed in the room adjoining Pierce's. The door was open, and during the night Pierce looked in on his sad, sick friend. Two hours later, his sleep interrupted by the bark of a local dog, Pierce checked again. Hawthorne hadn't moved. Pierce realized that he was dead.

Hawthorne's funeral at the end of May back in Concord was white with apple blossoms, scored by the calls of bobolinks and finches, and suffused with the smell of early lilacs. The Reverend James Freeman Clarke, who had married Hawthorne and Sophia, officiated. Emerson and Longfellow, Holmes and Whittier, Alcott and Louisa May, all followed the coffin to the Sleepy Hollow Cemetery, where Thoreau had been buried a few years before.

These days Plymouth, New Hampshire, is a small college town that you reach by turning off a wide straight road connecting with Interstate 93, which bisects New Hampshire from north to south. The dorms of Plymouth State University and the modern library dominate one side of the oval green, and a row of stores lines the other side. There's a curved wooden band shell and some pretty benches. Inside the county courthouse, a brick building with a broad staircase on the uphill side, hundreds of human dramas play out in front of the wide wooden bench of its courtroom. The railroad station is a little bit farther down the hill on Main Street, next to the movie theater. Until recently, the great white pile of the Pemigewasset House stood on a slight rise across the street. The hillside where my family has spent summers since the 1930s is just down the road.

One of the first trips I ever took was with my father to see the Old Manse in Concord, the house where Sophia carved their feelings into the upstairs glass with her diamond ring. Although I've been in Plymouth many times, I never knew that Hawthorne died there. I've been at the Plymouth Hospital too, first when my husband put a fishhook through his thumb, then when a nail hit me above the eye while my brother and I were dismantling a mouse-eaten mattress at the town dump, and the last time when I suffered flash burns on my cornea from windsurfing on Newfound Lake in the middle of the day. But it took me until last summer to go to the site of the old inn. It's gone now, but I remember it well. It was one of those New England white elephants bought by a series of optimistic families who hoped to restore it to its former grandeur and were defeated by the long winters and the short, short New Hampshire tourist season. The last time I stopped in there for an iced tea, it was run by an Indian family who had revamped the menu to include tandoori and curry.

Plymouth is a nice enough town, but it's not part of the blazing beauty of some sections of New Hampshire. It's too far south to be part of the White Mountains' gorgeous landscapes and too far north to be part of New Hampshire's jewely lake country. With its strip of malls and fake clapboard stores on the way out of town, and its camping store and bakery and health-food store with local produce in town, it's a town in the middle of nowhere, a town for people on the way to somewhere else.

47

LITTLE WOMEN

———◆———

Louisa May Alcott was a reluctant, rebellious thirty-six-year-old on the May morning in 1868 when she sat down to write *Little Women.* She worked at a small desk built in between two windows in her second-floor bedroom at Orchard House. A woolen shawl, worn over her usual brown muslin, warmed her against the drafts and the chill of New England. "Mr. Niles wants a girls' story, and I begin *Little Women,*" she wrote in her journal about her publisher's wish and the way in which it had become her command. "Marmee, Anna and May all approve my plan. So I plod away although I don't enjoy this sort of thing. Never liked girls or knew many, except my sisters, but our queer plays and experiences may prove interesting, though I doubt it."

In spite of her doubts, *Little Women,* which was to become one of the best-selling books of all time and end the Alcott family's decades of debilitating poverty, seemed to take hold of Louisa as she wrote. True, the writing of *Moods* had also taken hold of her in a similar way. She quickly realized that she had already written some pieces about her family among the dozens of magazine pieces she had published, and she wrote fast, without revision.

When she looked up during the day, past the rustic board fence her father had built at the edge of the property, she saw people and carriages passing on the Lexington Road and, beyond the road, pastures sparkling with wildflowers. When she wrote at night, by candlelight, she communed with a family of barred owls that lived in broad branches of the huge elm tree outside her windows.

As she wrote during the day, she could sometimes look down from the window and see her father, not working in the gardens behind the house, but sitting on the bench with a pile of his finest Red Pippin apples waiting for the occasional traveler who might be ready for a dose of his own brand of high philosophical discourse. Sometimes Emerson dropped by. Sometimes, Alcott would entertain a special visitor from Boston like Henry Wadsworth Longfellow, or Franklin Sanborn would wander up the Lexington Road to talk pedagogy, or one of the Hawthorne children would come over from next door. Beyond the meadows lay the shimmering water of Walden Pond, and the fields and marshes where Louisa had taken so many passionate walks so long ago with her teacher and friend Thoreau.

The little half-moon-shaped desk her father had built for her sat at the foot of Louisa's bed, surrounded by her books in a crowded cabinet bookcase, her sewing basket, family portraits, flower paintings by her older sister Anna, and a bust of the poet Schiller on the mantle. Although Orchard House was unheated except by fireplaces, and the Alcotts in later years often closed it up for the winter and moved to Boston, Louisa's room had a fireplace and windows facing south and west toward Concord. Her parents slept in the bedroom across the hall.

When she began writing *Little Women,* Louisa herself was still battling nervous exhaustion and arthritis brought on by the mercury poisoning as well as pains in her legs and back. Sometimes she was too weak to write. Sometimes she seemed to lose touch with who she was and what she was doing. Her right hand was beginning to cramp so painfully as she bore down on the metal pen nib and moved it over the paper that she would soon have to write with her left hand. Eventually, the mercury poisoning would kill her.

That spring, there were many other reasons for her to be discouraged. Her first serious novel had failed. As the culmination of decades of writing to order, editing others' work, teaching, and turning out the novelistic melodramas she called "rubbish" in order to alleviate the Alcotts' habitual poverty, it had held all her hopes for a literary career, and those hopes were once again dashed.

As she wrote at her second-floor windows, the last lilacs faded and the rhododendron bloomed. By June, after a month of writing day and night, she sent in twelve chapters of the book to Thomas Niles of Roberts Brothers, who was also her father's publisher. "He thought it dull," she wrote in her journal; "so do I." Nevertheless, she continued to work and by July 15 had completed the four-hundred-page manuscript that was the first part of *Little Women*. (The second part of the book was written later that year in another marathon writing session from October to January.)

By the time the hydrangeas bloomed in August, she was at her desk reading proofs. "It reads better than I expected," she wrote. "Not a bit sensational but simple and true, for we really lived most of it." Later, when the book began its extraordinary success, she expanded on this idea in a letter to another neighbor, Mary the wife of Colonel Thomas Wentworth Higginson—Emily Dickinson's editor and correspondent and one of John Brown's Secret Six. "The book was very hastily written to order & I had many doubts about the success of my first attempt at a girl's book," she wrote. "The characters were drawn from life, which gives them whatever merit they possess, for I find it impossible to invent anything half so true or touching as the simple facts with which everyday life supplies me."

But were they the facts? The difficulties, the debilitating poverty and claustrophobia of the Alcotts' life in Concord, become opportunities and closeness in the pages of *Little Women*. Sister Beth's horrifying and dreadful death from scarlet fever becomes a sweet and peaceful letting go. Louisa's furious jealousy at age thirty when her sister Anna married the penniless John Pratt becomes Jo's more normal teenage snit when her sister marries the adorable John Brooke. The family's grinding poverty, which had caused twenty moves in as many years, was transformed into friendly penny-pinching. The burden of running the household that fell largely on Louisa was shared in the fictional March household with a fictional loyal household retainer named Hannah. There was no Hannah in real life. The loss of Louisa's hair from disease in wartime became the noble sacrifice of Jo's hair to provide money to help her father when he was a soldier stricken with disease. (Jo's hair would quickly grow back. Louisa's would not.)

Most of all, Jo's rebelliousness in the book never keeps anyone from loving her, and in the end it serves her well. Jo is that rare thing, a rebel who somehow manages to be adored by the very people she's rebelling against. They understand her good intentions and love her for them. In real life, Louisa's rebelliousness made her a family outcast. Her father openly preferred her more conventional sisters. Her rebellion—her intelligence and her contrary nature—seems to have kept her from ever marrying or having her own family as Jo does. The book's energy comes from a fierce yearning, a longing to have had the fictional experience instead of the real one. *Little Women,* as many great books do, hovers in the gap between art and life—just alive enough so that we can recognize ourselves in its pages, just artistic enough so that we can find the lives we read about completely satisfying.

The huge success of *Little Women* changed the direction of Alcott's career, and for the remaining twenty years of her life she churned out best-selling sequels to the brilliant novel she wrote, almost by accident, in the spring of 1868. Although the money enabled her family to live comfortably, Alcott was never really resigned to her role as the beloved and celebrated author of her books for girls. She worried that she had become "a literary nursemaid providing moral pap for the young."

I first read *Little Women* when I was about ten. Like many women, I always wanted to be Jo. I was also the family rebel, the one who could never mind her manners, the one who was often angry, the one who was always pretending to be a horse when the time came to put on a dress and curtsy to Mrs. Frothingham. Most of the girls in the books I read—and in the life I led—were ladylike and pretty. Successful girls were thin and loved to wear nice clothes that always looked wonderful on them. On me, clothes always looked as if they belonged to someone else, and they often got torn and dirty on my excursions through the fields and woods around our house.

Jo March offered me a different kind of image, a new definition of what it meant to be a girl. Instead of a graceful young lady who always minded her manners and knew that her future lay in loving the right man, she was an outspoken, clumsy girl who turned down the right man even though he loved her.

Reading *Little Women* again, now, I can see how profoundly the book influenced me—as a woman, but even more than that as a writer. Without intending to, Louisa May Alcott invented a new way to write about the ordinary lives of women, and to tell stories that are usually heard in kitchens or bedrooms. She made literature out of the kind of conversations women have while doing the dishes together or taking care of their children. It was in *Little Women* that I learned that domestic details can be the subject of art, that small things in a woman's life— cooking, the trimming of a dress or hat, quiet talk—can be just as important a subject as a great whale or a scarlet letter. *Little Women* gave my generation of women permission to write about our daily lives; in many ways, even though it's a novel, in tone and voice it is the precursor of the modern memoir—the book that gives voice to people who have traditionally kept quiet. In fact, the foundation of the American memoir can be found in Alcott's masterpiece and in that of her friend Henry David Thoreau. Alcott's greatest work was so powerful because it was about ordinary things—I think that's why it felt ordinary even as she wrote it. She transformed the lives of women into something worthy of literature. Without even meaning to, Alcott exalted the everyday in women's lives and gave it greatness.

48

EMERSON AND THE FIRE

———◆———

As Emerson's health and energy declined, Lidian came into her own. Always a passionate gardener and well taught in naturalism by her friend Henry Thoreau, she now made friends in Concord through her extensive knowledge of gardening. Then on the night of July 23, 1872, Emerson suffered another loss in what felt like a string of losses. His last brother, William, was dead, his memory was failing, his energy flagging. Awakened in the upstairs bedroom by the sound of crackling, he saw that the house was on fire. The flames were visible in the next room.

He and Lidian opened a cupboard door and the fire roared out. Running to the front gate, Emerson shouted for help, and help came right away. Sam Staples, the man who had jailed Thoreau, took charge. A stream of neighbors carried out pictures, clothes, and furniture. By the time the town fire engine arrived and doused the flames, part of the house was still standing, but the ceilings and roof had collapsed. Emerson's study was spared, but the house would have to be rebuilt. The man who had financed so many others had finally run out of money himself. Painstakingly, he and friends moved the possessions of a lifetime from the lawn in front of the charred ruin a few blocks away to the courthouse.

Emerson, who moved into the empty Old Manse after the house where he had lived with his family for decades burned, was left the sad job of sorting through what was left. Insurance covered less than half. His friends in Concord rallied to raise thousands of dollars to rebuild the house and to send Emerson and his daughter Ellen on a long-dreamed-of trip to England, the Continent, and Egypt.

The fire seemed to take the life out of Emerson. His memory got much worse and it became hard for him to focus. He was sick all the time. His career as a lecturer was over. Traveling brought him back to life for a few days. "All this journey is a perpetual humiliation," he wrote in his journal after a trip up the Nile. "The people despise us because we are helpless babies who cannot speak or understand a word they say; the sphinxes scorn dunces; the obelisks, the temple walls defy us with their histories which we cannot spell."

In England in April, he wrote of the dutiful rounds of a famous man: "I saw Ferguson the architect; Browning the poet; John Stuart Mill; Sir Henry Holland; Huxley; Tyndall; Lord Houghton; Mr. Gladstone; Dean Stanley; Lecky; Froude; Thomas Hughes; Lyon Playfair; Sir Arthur Helps; the Duke of Argyle; the Duke of Bedford; the Duke of Cleveland." But his interest and intellect were gone. At dinners in London, he seated his son Edward, who was going to medical school in England, next to him in case he was unable to remember Lidian's name.

Concord mobilized her wealth to support the man of whom James Russell Lowell said, "When one meets him the Fall of Adam seems a false report." He had become an icon; even Harvard had put him on the prestigious Board of Overseers. While Emerson was abroad with his daughter, the friends and neighbors who had taken it upon themselves to support him were circulating a petition for funds to rebuild his house—handbills and fund-raising letters went to everyone in Concord and dozens of people in Boston. Money came in and the rebuilding started. As Emerson and Ellen went to parties in London, the sound of hammering and sawing and the swish of paintbrushes transformed the corner of the Cambridge Turnpike.

No one was sure which train would carry Emerson and Ellen from Boston to Concord after their boat from England landed in June, so the neighbors asked the engineers to signal with a whistle as they rolled along the downgrade from Walden Pond. At 3:30 P.M., the train whistle blew, and the bells of the town started ringing. A crowd including Lidian, the Alcotts, and Franklin Sanborn waited at the railroad station. The band played "Home Sweet Home." A dazed Emerson was escorted by cheering townspeople up past Monument Square and down toward his house. "Is this a public holiday?" he asked in bewilderment.

As they approached what he thought would be the charred ruin of his house, the town's schoolchildren were singing under an arch of apple boughs. The house had been rebuilt and restored exactly as it had been. It was as if the fire had never happened. All the efforts of the people who adored the seventy-year-old Emerson had managed to make every detail right. Emerson's journal entry on this day of celebration reflects his exhaustion. "Arrived Home at Concord, with Ellen & most kindly received by our townsmen & brought home to our rebuilt house." A house can be perfectly restored; a man cannot.

Emerson's Alzheimer's disease progressed, the plaques and tangles growing undetected in his brain, and there were many mortifying moments. When Mark Twain visited Boston at the invitation of William Dean Howells for a roast of a group of Brahmin intellectuals, he read a witty spoof of one of Emerson's most famous poems, *Brahma*. Emerson didn't laugh. Twain was baffled and embarrassed. "He never quite heard, never quite understood," wrote Ellen Emerson to Twain in a letter of explanation, "and he forgets easily and entirely."

Slowly, Emerson's life shut down. He spent days sitting at the desk in his study where so much of his life had happened. This was the room where he and Thoreau had their first conversation, the room where Margaret Fuller and he would talk for hours. An 1879 photograph shows the study unchanged but the man very changed. Emerson's once-tall frame is stooped over a book at his oblong desk. Hunched in a rocking chair with light streaming in from the glorious lawns and trees planted by Thoreau years before, he looks more posed than alive.

There were many visitors to the Emerson House as Emerson reached seventy-eight and then seventy-nine, but Lidian and Ellen took care of most of the conversations. Their son Edward came home to Concord and married Alice Keyes. Ellen lived in the house along with her mother.

On April 19, 1882—the day after the town's annual festival celebrating the American Revolution—Emerson went for a walk and got wet in a passing shower. He had a cold, which seemed to get worse.

The next morning on his way downstairs, he had what seemed to be a small stroke—he stumbled and cried out before recovering himself. He slept most of the day, and the next day the doctor diagnosed him as having pneumonia.

A day later, he got dressed as usual and went down to his study for tea. When he was finally persuaded to retire, he carefully closed up the study, the book-lined center of his universe. He shut each window and closed the shutters and then disassembled the fire for the night and walked slowly upstairs for the last time.

The Emerson family buried their patriarch in the Sleepy Hollow Cemetery on a ridge above town. There, perched even higher than the top of Author's Ridge where Thoreau, Hawthorne, and the Alcotts are buried, a monument of rose quartz dominates. Although it's hard to imagine Emerson choosing such a pride of place, he certainly belongs there. Without Emerson's dream of community—a dream all the more precious because of the shattering of his family and his expulsion from Harvard and the church—there would have been no American literary renaissance. There would have been no neighborhood where Margaret Fuller flirted with Nathaniel Hawthorne while enchanting his wife, and Henry David Thoreau took Louisa May Alcott for woodland walks. There would have been no Alcotts in Orchard House or Hawthornes at the Old Manse; there would have been no Thoreau at Walden, and no *Walden,* no *The Scarlet Letter,* or *Little Women.* There would have been no expression of the ideas that are still the credo of the environmental movement or the ideas that sparked feminism. Emerson's essays are small jewels that still gleam for the discerning reader, but his greatest contribution was in his life and the way he brought together, supported, and encouraged the community that became Concord, Massachusetts.

Louisa May Alcott lived another twenty years after the publication and wild success of *Little Women.* They were years of travel and abundance, but years in which the mercury that had poisoned her system never gave up its hold. She continued to live in Orchard House with her parents and whichever sisters needed a place to stay. Her fame may have changed the way she was seen by the world, but that and her financial success didn't change her relationship to the world of her intimate friends. When her father died on March 4, 1888, long ago forgiven for his flightiness by his practical daughter, she was overwhelmed by the arrangements she, as usual, had to make. "Shall I ever find time to die?" she wrote, a final complaint from the woman who had spent her life and her time bending to others' needs. Two days later she did, dying on March 6 in her sleep.

CONCORD, TODAY

———◆———

I had been reading about Concord, Massachusetts, in the 1840s and '50s for about a year before I first managed to actually visit. I had been in Concord before, as a child in the 1950s and visiting a friend in the 1970s. I had read many books about the Concord writers and their American renaissance. A few years ago, these two things—the place and the literature—began to knit themselves together in my imagination.

Pretty soon I was obsessed with Concord in the 1850s. I lived there in my mind as much as I could between taking my son to school and teaching and writing. Every evening I would retreat to my Concord, reliving the sorrows of the Emerson household or the dizzy hopes of Louisa May Alcott.

When I finally got there, it was a hot August day and I had a car full of children—my son, my daughter, and a friend—as well as two panting dogs—a corgi and a dachshund. My brain simmered as I drove down Route 2 from New York en route to New Hampshire for my first view of the place I had been living in my imagination. What a shock. Somehow, I had thought I would be driving into the nineteenth century. Instead of the few shops along the Milldam and the clip-clop of horses' hooves, I was halted a mile out of town by a traffic jam. By the time I got to Monument Square, the occupants of the car were in rebellion. There was nowhere to park. One of the dogs started whining. When I finally found a parking space, everyone piled out of the car onto the molten pavement and into the crowds of unfriendly tourists. Where were the Alcotts? Where was Thoreau who should have been shambling down Main Street with a walking stick? There was nothing to see and everything to buy.

Unfamiliar with this town, which in its reality seemed as foreign to me as the most remote corners of the earth, I was unable to find an ice-cream store or a bathroom or any of the other amenities, which are required by children on long trips. We piled back into the car and drove toward the crossroads where American literature was written. At least in front of the Emerson House, there was somewhere to park and let out the dogs on the grass. No one was happy. The possibility of going inside the Emerson House seemed remote with three children and two dogs, and I began to lose my hold on the delicious small town of my memory. Where was the Concord I had hoped to write about?

Back in the car, now crowded with children and dogs complaining vocally, I announced that we would at least go and see the Old North Bridge. "It's your heritage!" I commanded. I had lost my book, but I wasn't about to lose this battle.

At the Old Manse, the parking lot was crammed with school buses; crowds of children and families filled the path to the Old North Bridge. My children refused to get out of the car.

It took a month to reassemble in my imagination the images of my Concord—the Concord where Hawthorne and Thoreau rode the ice floe, and where Emerson was jealous of Hawthorne.

At first, every visit to modern Concord dissipated my book, which had to be reassembled with the library I was building at home in New York. Staying at the Best Western built on a pasture near Fairhaven Bay and breakfasting with businessmen, the Concord I loved seemed worlds away. But as the months and years went by, I began to have a few moments that matched.

One February, staying at the Colonial Inn—Shattuck's Store to the Alcotts—when the town was empty, I had a sense that I had gone back in time. Looking out my narrow window at Monument Square toward the steep white spire of the Unitarian Church, I could almost see Hawthorne and Margaret Fuller with their backs to me as they walked and talked on their way to the Emerson House. Her skirts billowed out in the breeze; he leaned over to hear her better. As they passed the end of the square, they both burst out laughing at some private joke. One evening walking down the fields below the Old Manse where the mossy bank drops into the river, I just missed Hawthorne on his way down from the house to take a cooling swim.

In a canoe on the Sudbury and Assabet rivers one summer afternoon, I saw something Thoreau would have loved. Gliding up past the meadows where the smells of grass and wildflowers lay in the still air, a friend and I came upon a great horned owl that appeared to be wounded. The large owl was trying to fly and failing, splashing with a *whoosh* down into the water after a few feet. As we approached as silently as possible, the owl's attempts became more desperate. Each time the owl took off, he cleared the water by less and less until the bird was actually swimming a kind of painful breaststroke in front of the canoe. As our eyes adjusted, we saw that the owl was not wounded. He was holding his dinner—a muskrat—and the weight of the rat was keeping the bird from flying. Suddenly, the owl dropped the rat, glided upward, and sat on a dead log in perfect camouflage to let us pass. Later, when we paddled back downstream toward home, the owl was enjoying his dinner in the tall reeds at the side of the river.

I began to see that the sepia tones of the Concord of my imagination were still there, hidden under the bright colors of the stores and cars of modern-day Concord. It was a subtler place, and sometimes hard to find. In the re-creation of Emerson's study at the Concord Museum, I felt it for a moment, and one afternoon on the shores of Walden Pond. Slowly, the book began to assemble itself, and I began to see the Alcotts arriving in front of the house where the Middlesex Hotel once stood, and the Hawthorne family leaving the Old Manse in a carriage, with nowhere to go. This book is taken from that imagined landscape, the landscape of a Concord where five people tangled with each other and the world and wrote the books that still inspire us. It is my hope that this story will serve as an introduction to that landscape and that the reader will come to love it as I have.

CHRONOLOGY

———◆———

1838: Ralph Waldo Emerson marries his second wife, Lydia Jackson, and moves to Concord, Massachusetts.

1840: The Alcotts—Bronson, Abba, and their daughters, including Louisa May—arrive in Concord. Both Thoreau brothers—Henry David and John—propose to the young Ellen Sewall, both are rejected. Margaret Fuller begins editing Emerson's magazine, *The Dial*.

1841: Nathaniel Hawthorne goes to Brook Farm. Margaret Fuller visits Brook Farm. Henry David Thoreau moves in to the Emerson House in Concord.

1842: Bronson Alcott goes to England. John Thoreau dies of lockjaw. Waldo Emerson dies. Hawthorne marries Sophia Peabody on July 9, and they move to Concord.

1843: The Alcotts go to Fruitlands. Thoreau goes to New York.

1844: Fruitlands fails. Una Hawthorne is born in Concord. Margaret Fuller moves to New York to work at the *New York Tribune*.

1845: The Alcotts buy a house in Concord and name it Hillside. Thoreau goes back to live on Walden Pond. The Hawthornes are kicked out of Concord and go back to Salem. Margaret Fuller publishes *Woman in the Nineteenth Century*.

1846: Margaret Fuller sails to Europe, meets Carlyle and Mazzini.

1847: Thoreau leaves Walden and moves back into the Emerson House. Emerson takes his second trip to Europe. Fuller moves to Rome, meets Giovanni Angelo Ossoli and becomes his lover.

1848: The Alcotts move to Boston. Emerson travels abroad. In Rieti, Italy, Margaret Fuller gives birth on September 5 to Angelo Eugenio Filippo Ossoli, called Nino.

1849: Thoreau's first book is published. Fuller, Ossoli, and the baby move to Florence.

1850: Hawthorne publishes *The Scarlet Letter* and leaves Salem. In Stockbridge, he meets Herman Melville. Margaret Fuller, Ossoli, and the baby embark from Italy on the *Elizabeth* on May 17.

1852: The Hawthornes leave Stockbridge and eventually buy the Alcotts' house in Concord, renaming it Wayside.

1853: Hawthorne is appointed Americal consul to Liverpool.

1854: In Boston, editor James Fields tells Louisa May Alcott she can't write. *Walden* is published.

1855: The Alcotts move to Walpole, New Hampshire.

1856: Thoreau meets Walt Whitman.

1857: The Alcotts return to Concord buying Orchard House, next to Wayside. Thoreau meets John Brown.

1858: Lizzie Alcott dies. Anna Alcott marries John Pratt, the son of Minot Pratt, the director of Brook Farm. The Hawthornes travel from Liverpool to France and Italy.

1859: John Brown speaks in Concord again. Brown is executed in December after his attack on Harper's Ferry in October.

1860: Louisa May Alcott begins work on her novel *Moods*. The Hawthornes return to Wayside. Thoreau climbs Mount Monadnock with Ellery Channing.

1862: Thoreau dies of tuberculosis on May 6. Louisa May Alcott goes to Washington and works as a nurse for Dorothea Dix at the Union Hotel Hospital.

1863: After severe illness, Louisa May Alcott returns home, begins publishing *Hospital Sketches* as letters about her nursing experience.

1864: *Moods* is published. Hawthorne dies in Plymouth, New Hampshire.

1865: Louisa meets Henry James; he gives *Moods* a bad review. Louisa goes to Europe.

1867: Thomas Niles commissions Louisa May Alcott to write a story for girls. She resists.

1868: In a February article, Louisa May Alcott writes that "Liberty is a better husband than love to many of us." In May and June, she reluctantly writes *Little Women*.

1869: Louisa May Alcott pays off the family debts.

1872: Emerson House burns down on July 24.

1879: May Alcott Nieriker dies in Europe, Louisa adopts her daughter, Lulu.

1882: Louisa May Alcott helps found a temperance society in Concord. Emerson dies on April 27.

1888: Bronson Alcott dies on March 4. Louisa May Alcott dies two days later.

ACKNOWLEDGMENTS

Every book is a collaberation, and a biography of five writers is an extreme example. My greatest debt is to my subjects and teachers, the courageous Louisa May
Alcott; the generous and revolutionary Emerson; the brilliant Hawthorne; the
angry, principled Thoreau; and the glamorous Margaret Fuller. During the six
years I have been obsessed with these people, many friends and acquaintances
have helped by being open to passionate discussions of nineteenth-century behavior and gossip about a few long-ago incidents. They have responded to my unrea-
sonable interest with patience and encouragement.

For just listening, I want to thank first of all my daughter, Sarah, and my son,
Quad, who were with me on many trips to Concord and who—sometimes reluc-
tantly—joined me in my search for the past. I also want to thank Adam Bock;
Blake Bailey; Tina Brown and Harry Evans; Ken Burrows and Erica Jong; my
brother Ben, who is my close friend and esteemed colleague; Amy Belding
Brown; Ned Cabot; Judy Collins; June Iseman; Ron Gallen; Eliza Griswold; the
Right Reverend Frank Griswold and Phoebe Griswold; Skip Gates; Jane
Hirschfield; Warren Hinckle III; Jane Hitchcock; Mary-Beth Hughes; Molly
Jong-Fast and Matt Greenfield; Jeanette Watson Sanger, who inadvertently
inspired this book in the first place; Muriel Lloyd; Fran Liebowitz; Ken Lauber;
J. B. Miller; Rick Moody, Hannah and Gavin McFarland; Gardner McFall;
Ruthie Rogers; Maggie Scarf; Bill Vinyard; Kathy Rich; Reba White Williams;
and Rob Perkins, who was, for one sunlit afternoon, my personal Thoreau.

I also am indebted to the staff of the Colonial Inn and the staff of the Best
Western hotel in Concord; John and Charlotte Kenney, for their extraordinary
hospitality and scholarship; the Point O' Woods Library; the Houghton Library
at Harvard University; and the Concord Free Library and its Special Collections
curator Leslie Perrin Wilson.

I am indebted to the professionals who kept my body and soul together while
I researched and wrote. Dr. Bruce Yaffe and his colleagues, Dr. Murray Brennan

and Dr. Theodore Jacobs, as well as the wonderful men and women who helped raise my children and keep them healthy—the teachers and administrators at the Rudolf Steiner School, Princeton University, and the Law School of the University of the District of Columbia, Dr. Natalie Geary, and Stuart and Simon and the guys at Games Workshop.

At Simon & Schuster, I have had the inestimable support and help of Michael Korda, Chuck Adams, Sydny Miner, the legendary Gypsy "Spitfire" da Silva, Mike Hill, Fred Wiemer, Dahlia Adler, Anthony Newfield, and Victoria Meyer. Without my brilliant literary agents, Kim Witherspoon and David Forrer, this book would never have been written.

I also want to thank my beloved colleagues at Bennington led by the raffish but elegant Liam Rector, especially Nuala O'Faolain, Amy Hempel, Sheila Kohler, Sven Birkerts, Cilla Hodgkins, Tom Bissell, Lyndall Gordon, the divine Jill McCorkle, the great Bob Shacochis, and my esteemed colleagues at The New School, Robert Polito, Jackson Taylor, and Susannah Lessard.

Without the enchanted rooms at Yaddo, where time stops and writing seems to have an energy of its own, and where the imagined past is as vivid as the real present, I would not have been able to write this book.

NOTES

Writing about writers is always a thrill, and the writers with whom I have had the privilege of sojourning in this book are some of the most thrilling who have ever appeared in print. Reading and rereading their work is a pleasure—especially *Walden, Little Women, The Scarlet Letter,* and *Moby-Dick.* These are among the most enjoyable books ever written, and in their scope and imagination they are the precursors of most of American literature, from the memoir to nature writing to the narrative that pits man against nature. The brilliant aphorisms embedded in Emerson's essays, Thoreau's sublime sentence structure and observation of detail, Hawthorne's ability to spin fictional gold from the straw of everyday experience, and Louisa May Alcott's illumination of the details of women's lives all inspired me as I read about these writers and studied their work. Henry James's biography of Nathaniel Hawthorne, arguably the first American literary biography, was another rich starting point. So in reflecting on the sources of this book, I would have to say that the first source, the Ur-source, the imaginative powerhouse from which my energy came, is the brilliant writing of my five subjects, which I have quoted wherever possible.

I first encountered the premise of this book in an American literature course at Brown University back in the 1960s in which we studied F. O. Matthiessen's brilliant *American Renaissance,* a book about Thoreau, Emerson, Hawthorne, Melville, and Whitman. Over the years, I've read dozens of books about the extraordinary events in and around Concord, Massachusetts, in the years between 1840 and the Civil War, from Van Wyck Brooks's *The Flowering of New England* through Lawrence Buell and Perry Miller, Robert Richardson and Carlos Baker and Philip McFarland, Megan Marshall and James R. Mellow. Recently, novels with the Emersons or the Alcotts as main characters, such as those by Geraldine Brooks and Amy Belding Brown, have added another dimension to the writing about this extraordinary cluster of geniuses. Much of this writing is brilliant, and although some of these books aren't mentioned in the endnotes, they are also sources of this book and their writers the teachers who made it possible.

Although I spent wonderful hours at the Houghton Library at Harvard University, the most generous and elegant research library I can imagine, the real spirit of the scenes in my book came from something simpler than library work—going to the places the men and women went and doing what they did. Breathing in the warm summer air in the marshes of the upper reaches of the Assabet as Thoreau did, looking out on the landscape of the woods and fields from the second story of Orchard House as Louisa May Alcott did, watching evening fall on the pasture next to the Old Manse as Hawthorne and his young bride Sophia Peabody did, took me back more than a hundred years. Through good fortune and local conservation efforts, many of the Concord landscapes are hardly changed from the time when Emerson and Thoreau walked across Monument Square to pay the Hawthornes a visit. The trees have grown so that the pasture where Thoreau built his hut on Walden Pond is now a thick grove that shades the pile of stones left by visiting pilgrims. The Old North Bridge, which was washed away, has now been replaced. Still in the early morning, or when the late afternoon sun slants right through the waters of the Concord River to the grasses at the bottom, time stops and the worlds of the present and the past come together in the landscapes—inner and outer—that I have tried to bring to life in this book.

I have used the following abbreviations:

RWE—Ralph Waldo Emerson
NH—Nathaniel Hawthorne
LMA—Louisa May Alcott
HDT—Henry David Thoreau

PART 1

PAGE

9 *"we will call on his aid as we often do"*: RWE, writing about Bronson Alcott in a letter to Sophia Peabody, quoted in James R. Mellow, *Nathaniel Hawthorne in His Times,* p. 173.

10 *"I want my place, my own place, my true place"*: NH, as quoted in Paul Brooks, *The People of Concord,* p. 8 (Brooks has no note on this quotation).

11 *"Transcendental forms . . . whatever belongs"*: RWE, in his essay "The Transcendentalist," in *The Essential Writings of Ralph Waldo Emerson,* p. 86.

15 *"Alcott's combination of manual labor"*: W. E. Channing to Elizabeth Peabody, as quoted in Carlos Baker, *Emerson Among the Eccentrics,* p. 177.

32 *"she was thought to have the power"*: An obituary of Mary Moody Emerson from the *Boston Commonwealth,* quoted in Robert Richardson, *Emerson,* p. 23.

40 *nicked the ring finger of his left hand:* Walter Harding, *The Days of Henry Thoreau,* on the death of John Thoreau, p. 134.

51 *"Thoreau, who has a strange faculty of finding"*: NH, in *Mosses from an Old Manse,* p. 9.

53 *"Then we talked about Autumn"*: NH, *The American Notebooks,* ed. Claude

Simpson (Columbus: Ohio State University Press, 1972), p. 342, quoted in
Bell Gale Chevigny, *The Woman and the Myth,* p. 161.

PART 2

PAGE

66 *"The scholar not infrequently envies the propriety": The Journal of Henry David Thoreau,* vol. 1, p. 313.

68 *Royall's daughter:* Megan Marshall, *The Peabody Sisters,* p. 30.

72 *"It brings the noisy world":* (July 27, 1844) NH, in the *Centenary Edition of the Works of Nathaniel Hawthorne* (Columbus: Ohio State University Press, 1962–1997), vol. 8, p. 248, quoted in James R. Mellow, *Nathaniel Hawthorne in His Times,* p. 244.

72 *"I can remember": The Journal of Henry David Thoreau,* April 3, 1842, vol. 1, p. 358.

75 *There they carefully built:* Walter Harding, *The Days of Henry Thoreau,* p. 161; and Robert Richardson, *Henry David Thoreau,* p. 144.

78 *"Where'er thou sail'st":* Henry David Thoreau, *A Week on the Concord and Merrimack Rivers,* epigraph.

80 "Thoreau's Sexuality": *Journal of Homosexuality,* vol. 21, no. 3 (1991).

81 *"In looking for the causes of the great influence":* Sarah Freeman Clarke, as quoted by Thomas Wentworth Higginson, cited in Bell Gale Chevigny, *The Woman and the Myth,* p. 87.

82 *"He apotheosized her as the greatest":* NH, letters to Sophia in April of 1842, quoted in James R. Mellow, *Nathaniel Hawthorne in His Times,* p. 225.

83 *"Waldo was here three times yesterday":* Margaret Fuller's Journals, quoted in Bell Gale Chevigny, *The Woman and the Myth,* p. 550.

83 *"Was I not raised":* RWE, *Journals and Miscellaneous Notebooks,* 1840.

86 *"We were actually turned out of roof and home":* Sophia Hawthorne to Louisa Hawthorne, quoted in Brenda Wineapple, *Hawthorne: A Life,* p. 190.

87 *"We gathered up our household goods":* NH, quoted in James R. Mellow, *Nathaniel Hawthorne in His Times,* p. 265.

88 *"The American authoress, Miss Fuller":* Elizabeth Barrett Browning, quoted in Carlos Baker, *Emerson Among the Eccentrics,* p. 317.

91 *"small sneers at Salem":* James R. Mellow, *Nathaniel Hawthorne in His Times,* p. 316.

99 *"Hawthorne was a fastidious man":* Brenda Wineapple, *Hawthorne: A Life,* p. 228.

102 *"The town is full of Irish":* RWE to HDT, in Robert Richardson, *Henry David Thoreau,* p. 138 (no note).

102 *"Wherever that music comes":* James R. Mellow, *Nathaniel Hawthorne in His Times,* quoting RWE, *Journals and Miscellaneous Notebooks,* vol. 7, p. 482 (with thanks to Leo Marx and his book *The Machine in the Garden*), p. 244. Mellow also quotes NH, who hears the train whistle at about 10 A.M. on July

27, 1844, and finds it harsh: "It tells the story of busy men ... it brings the noisy world into our slumberous peace."

106 *"Carlyle indeed is arrogant":* Paula Blanchard, *Margaret Fuller,* p. 258.

107 *"Can you not safely take the first steamer":* RWE to Margaret Fuller, quoted in Carlos Baker, *Emerson Among the Eccentrics,* p. 298 (no note).

108 *"Henry David Thoreau is like the wood God":* RWE, *Journals and Miscellaneous Notebooks,* quoted in Robert Richardson, *Emerson,* p. 462.

PART 3

PAGE

130 *"Why did I leave the woods":* HDT, *The Journal of Henry David Thoreau,* quoted in Henry Salt, *The Life of Henry David Thoreau,* p. 50.

132 *"If I could save the Union without freeing any slave":* President Abraham Lincoln, *The Collected Works of Abraham Lincoln,* ed. Roy P. Basler, vol. 5, p. 388, quoted in Philip McFarland, *Hawthorne in Concord,* p. 269.

136 *"I have enjoyed many bright peaceful hours":* Bell Gale Chevigny, *The Woman and the Myth.*

136 *"Should I never return":* Ibid., p. 477.

137 *"For me, I long so very much":* Ibid.

137 *"Rainy weather delays us now":* Ibid., p. 496.

142 *"I dread to speak of Margaret":* Sophia Hawthorne to her mother, August 1, 1850, quoted in James R. Mellow, *Nathaniel Hawthorne in His Times,* p. 329 (Sophia wrote a similar letter to her sister Mary Mann on September 9). (Letters are in the Berg Collection of the New York Public Library.)

145 *"He thinks a good deal":* Ellery Channing to Ellen Channing, October 30, 1851, Massachusetts Historical Society, quoted in James R. Mellow, *Nathaniel Hawthorne in His Times,* p. 381.

145 *Now in the Berkshires:* The story of Hawthorne's apples taken from the Tappan tree and the wedge it drove between the two families may sound improbable, but I remember living in a ruin of a castle in Porto Ercole, Italy, in 1956 when a similar fight broke out around some figs we children had picked off a tree that, as it turned out, belonged—or was thought by her to belong—to the castle's longtime concierge. The fight began in the morning; we were gone by dinnertime. The friendship between my father and Eleanor Clark, who had previously lived in the castle and brokered the rental, and her husband, Robert Penn Warren, never quite recovered from the incident of the figs.

146 *"Before Mr. Alcott took it in hand":* NH to George William Curtis, quoted in Henry James, *Hawthorne,* p. 110 (the Henry James biography of Hawthorne has no endnotes).

151 *"in his presence one feels ashamed":* NH, quoted in Randall Stewart, *Nathaniel Hawthorne,* p. 142 (Stewart has no endnotes).

154 *"unjustifiable intellectual aristocracy":* From Victor Channing Sanborn's

memoir of Franklin Sanborn in the Sanborn Family Papers at the Boston Public Library, quoted in Edward Renehan, *The Secret Six,* p. 109.

156 *"Something is going to be done":* John Brown, as quoted in David S. Reynolds, *John Brown, Abolitionist,* p. 158.

158 *"Thoreau and Emerson took John Brown":* Robert Penn Warren, *John Brown,* p. 245.

160 *"The execution of St. John the Just":* Louisa May Alcott's journals, quoted in James R. Mellow, *Nathaniel Hawthorne in His Times,* p. 535.

160 *"Think much of Capt Brown":* Amos Bronson Alcott's Journals, October 30 and 31, 1859, quoted in Carlos Baker, *Emerson Among the Eccentrics,* p. 385.

160 *"When I said that I thought he was right":* HDT, *The Journal of Henry David Thoreau,* 1860, p. 292.

161 *"This will be a great day":* Letters of Oliver Wendell Holmes, quoted in Robert Penn Warren, *John Brown,* p. 437.

162 *"Most of the people who sat about him":* Robert Penn Warren, *John Brown,* p. 314.

163 *"I think there prevailed":* RWE, *Historic Notes of Life and Letters in New England,* in *The Transcendentalists,* an anthology edited by Perry Miller, p. 501.

PART 4

PAGE

171 *"The country through which we passed":* Louisa May Alcott, *Hospital Sketches,* p. 22.

182 *"Nobody was ever more justly hanged":* Centenary Edition of the *Works of Nathaniel Hawthorne,* vol. 12, p. 328, quoted in James R. Mellow, *Nathaniel Hawthorne in His Times,* p. 551.

182 *"New England will still have her rocks":* NH to Henry Bright, December 17, 1860, Beinecke Library, Yale University Collection of American Literature, quoted in James R. Mellow, *Nathaniel Hawthorne in His Times,* p. 536.

183 *"How can you tell anything":* Sophia Peabody Hawthorne to Elizabeth Peabody, Berg Collection of the New York Public Library, quoted in James R. Mellow, *Nathaniel Hawthorne in His Times,* p. 535.

184 *"If he is so exceedingly unpopular":* NH to James Fields, July 18, 1863, Houghton Library Collection, quoted in James R. Mellow, *Nathaniel Hawthorne in His Times,* p. 566.

186 *"OWH thinks the shark's tooth is on him":* From M. A. DeWolfe Howe, *Memories of a Hostess,* p. 27, quoted in James R. Mellow, *Nathaniel Hawthorne in His Times,* p. 576.

195 *"All this journey is a perpetual humiliation":* RWE, *The Heart of Emerson's Journals,* p. 335.

196 *"Arrived Home at Concord":* The Letters of Ralph Waldo Emerson quoted in Carlos Baker, *Emerson Among the Eccentrics,* p. 515.

BIBLIOGRAPHY

———

Alcott, Louisa May. *Behind a Mask: The Unknown Thrillers of Louisa May Alcott.* Edited by Madeleine Stern. New York: Quill/William Morrow, 1995.

———. *Hospital Sketches.* Bedford, Mass.: Applewood Books, 1993.

———. *The Inheritance.* New York: Penguin, 1997.

———. *Little Women.* With an introduction by Susan Cheever. New York: Modern Library Paperback, 2000.

———. *Louisa May Alcott: Her Life, Letters, and Journals.* Edited by Ednah D. Cheney. Boston: Little, Brown, 1928.

———. *Louisa May Alcott Unmasked: Collected Thrillers.* Edited by Madeleine Stern. Boston: Northeastern University Press, 1995.

———. *Moods.* New Brunswick, N.J.: Rutgers University Press, 1991.

———. *The Selected Letters of Louisa May Alcott.* Edited by Joel Myerson, Daniel Shealy, and Madeleine B. Stern. Boston: Little, Brown, 1987.

———. *Transcendental Wild Oats and Excerpts from the Fruitlands Diary.* Harvard, Mass.: Harvard Common Press, 1981.

Allen, Gay Wilson. *Melville and His World.* New York: Viking, 1971.

Andrews, Joseph L., Jr. *Revolutionary Boston, Lexington, and Concord: The Shots Heard 'Round the World!* Beverly, Mass.: Commonwealth Editions, 2002.

Baker, Carlos. *Emerson Among the Eccentrics: A Group Portrait.* New York: Viking, 1996.

Beecher, Catherine E., and Harriet Beecher Stowe. *The American Woman's Home.* Hartford, Conn.: Harriet Beecher Stowe Center, 2002.

Blanchard, Paula. *Margaret Fuller: From Transcendentalism to Revolution.* Reading, Mass.: Addison-Wesley, 1987.

Bonfanti, Leo. *Biographies and Legends of the New England Indians.* Vols. 1–2. Burlington, Mass.: Pride Publications, 1970.

Botkin, B. A., ed. *A Treasury of New England Folklore.* New York: Bonanza Books, 1995.

Brooks, Geraldine. *March.* New York: Viking, 2005.

Brooks, Paul. *The People of Concord: One Year in the Flowering of New England.* Chester, Conn.: Glove Pequot Press, 1990.

Brooks, Van Wyck. *The Flowering of New England, 1815–1865.* New York: Dutton, 1936.

Buell, Lawrence. *Emerson.* Cambridge, Mass.: Belknap Press of Harvard University Press, 2003.

———. *The Environmental Imagination: Thoreau, Nature Writing, and the Formation of American Culture.* Cambridge, Mass.: Belknap Press of Harvard University Press, 1995.

———. *Literary Transcendentalism: Style and Vision in the American Renaissance.* Ithaca, N.Y.: Cornell University Press, 1973.

———. *New England Literary Culture from the Revolution to the Renaissance.* Cambridge: Cambridge University Press, 1986.

Chapin, Sarah. *Concord, Massachusetts.* Charleston, S.C.: Arcadia Publishing, 1997.

Chevigny, Bell Gale. *The Woman and the Myth: Margaret Fuller's Life and Writings.* Boston: Northeastern University Press, 1994.

Dawes, Claiborne; Sarah Chapin; and Alice Moulton. *Concord.* Charleston, S.C.: Arcadia Publishing, 2001.

De Graaf, Richard M., and Mariko Yamasaki, eds. *New England Wildlife.* Hanover, N.H.: University Press of New England, 2001.

Delano, Sterling F. *Brook Farm: The Dark Side of Utopia.* Cambridge, Mass.: Belknap Press of Harvard University Press, 2004.

Emerson, Ralph Waldo. *The Essential Writings of Ralph Waldo Emerson.* Edited by Brooks Atkinson. New York: Modern Library, 2000.

———. *The Heart of Emerson's Journals.* Edited by Bliss Perry. Boston: Houghton Mifflin, 1914.

———. *Self-Reliance and Other Essays.* New York: Barnes & Noble, 1995.

Frothingham, Octavius Brooks. *Transcendentalism in New England.* New York: Harper & Brothers, 1959.

Fuller, Margaret. *My Heart Is a Large Kingdom: Selected Letters of Margaret Fuller.* Edited by Robert N. Hudspeth. Ithaca, N.Y.: Cornell University Press, 2001.

———. *Woman in the Nineteenth Century.* Mineola, N.Y.: Dover Publications, 1999.

Harding, Walter. *The Days of Henry Thoreau: A Biography.* New York: Dover Publications, 1982.

Hawthorne, Nathaniel. *Collected Novels.* New York: Library of America, 1983.

———. *The House of the Seven Gables.* With an introduction by Mary Oliver. New York: Modern Library, 2001.

———. *Mosses from an Old Manse.* New York: Modern Library, 2003.

———. *The Scarlet Letter.* New York: Barnes & Noble, 2001.

———. *Twenty Days with Julian and Little Bunny by Papa.* New York: New York Review of Books, 2003.

James, Henry. *Hawthorne.* Ithaca, N.Y.: Cornell University Press, 1997.

Keynes, John Maynard. *The Economic Consequences of the Peace.* New York: Harcourt, Brace and Howe, 1920.

King, B. A. *Snow Season.* New London, N.H.: Safe Harbor Books, 2001.

Kornfeld, Eve. *Margaret Fuller: A Brief Biography with Documents.* Boston: Bedford Books, 1997.

Langton, Jane. *God in Concord.* New York: Penguin, 1992.

Leech, Margaret. *Reveille in Washington, 1860–1865.* Alexandria, Va., 1980.

Marshall, Megan. *The Peabody Sisters: Three Women Who Ignited American Romanticism.* Boston: Houghton Mifflin, 2005.

Matthiessen, F. O. *American Renaissance.* New York: Oxford University Press, 1968.

McAdow, Ron. *The Concord, Sudbury, and Assabet Rivers: A Guide to Canoeing, Wildlife, and History.* Illustrated by Gordon Morrison. Marlborough, Mass.: Bliss Publishing Co., 1990.

McFarland, Philip. *Hawthorne in Concord.* New York: Grove, 2004.

McMurry, Andrew. *Environmental Renaissance: Emerson, Thoreau, and the Systems of Nature.* Athens: University of Georgia Press, 2003.

Mellow, James R. *Nathaniel Hawthorne in His Times.* Boston: Houghton Mifflin, 1980.

Meltzer, Milton, and Walter Harding. *A Thoreau Profile.* New York: Thomas Y. Crowell & Co., 1962.

Miller, Perry. *The American Puritans.* Garden City, N.Y.: Doubleday, 1956.

———, ed. *The Transcendentalists.* Cambridge, Mass.: Harvard University Press, 1950.

Mitchell, John Hanson. *Walking Towards Walden: A Pilgrimage in Search of Place.* Reading, Mass.: Addison-Wesley, 1995.

Moody, Rick. *The Black Veil.* Boston: Little, Brown, 2002.

Nasar, Sylvia. *A Beautiful Mind.* London and New York: Faber & Faber, 1998.

Novak, Barbara. *The Ape and the Whale: An Interplay Between Darwin and Melville in Their Own Words.* Moose, Wyo.: Homestead Publishing, 1995.

———. *The Margaret-Ghost.* New York: George Braziller, 2003.

Peabody, Elizabeth Palmer. *The Letters of Elizabeth Palmer Peabody.* Edited by Bruce A. Ronda. Middletown, Conn.: Wesleyan University Press, 1984.

Philbrick, Nathaniel. *In the Heart of the Sea.* New York: Viking, 2000.

———. *Sea of Glory: America's Voyage of Discovery: The U.S. Exploring Expedition, 1838–1842.* New York: Viking, 2003.

Renehan, Edward J., Jr. *The Secret Six: The True Tale of the Men Who Conspired with John Brown.* New York: Crown, 1995.

Reynolds, David S. *John Brown, Abolitionist.* New York: Knopf, 2005.

Richardson, Robert D., Jr. *Emerson: The Mind on Fire.* Berkeley: University of California Press, 1995.

———. *Henry David Thoreau: A Life of the Mind.* Berkeley: University of California Press, 1986.

Salt, Henry S. *Life of Henry David Thoreau.* Urbana: University of Illinois Press, 1993.

Saxton, Martha. *Louisa May Alcott: A Modern Biography*. New York: Farrar, Straus & Giroux, 1995.

Scudder, Townsend. *Concord: American Town*. Boston: Little, Brown, 1947.

Sewall, Richard B. *The Life of Emily Dickinson*. Cambridge, Mass.: Harvard University Press, 1980.

Shenk, David. *The Forgetting: Alzheimer's: Portrait of an Epidemic*. New York: Doubleday, 2001.

Smith, Harmon. *My Friend, My Friend: The Story of Thoreau's Relationship with Emerson*. Amherst: University of Massachusetts Press, 1999.

Stearns, Frank Preston. *Sketches from Concord and Appledore*. New York: Putnam, 1895.

Stern, Madeleine B. *Louisa May Alcott*. Boston: Northeastern University Press, 1999.

Stewart, Randall. *Nathaniel Hawthorne: A Biography*. New Haven, Conn.: Yale University Press, 1948.

Strickland, Charles. "A Transcendentalist Father: The Child-Rearing Practices of Bronson Alcott." *Perspectives in American History*, vol. 3 (1969), pp. 5–73.

Tharp, Louise Hall. *The Peabody Sisters of Salem*. Boston: Little, Brown, 1951.

Thoreau, Henry David. *Cape Cod*. With an introduction by Robert Pinsky. Princeton, N.J.: Princeton University Press, 2004.

———. *Consciousness in Concord: The Text of Thoreau's "Lost Journal," 1840–1841, Together with Notes and a Commentary by Perry Miller*. Boston: Houghton Mifflin. 1958.

———. *The Journal of Henry David Thoreau*. Vols. 1–7. Salt Lake City: Peregrine Smith Books, 1984.

———. *Thoreau on Birds: Notes on New England Birds from the Journals of Henry David Thoreau*. Edited by Francis Allen; illustrated by Louis Agassiz Fuertes. Boston: Beacon Press, 1993.

———. *Walden*. New York: Barnes & Noble, 1993.

———. *Walden*. An annotated edition edited by Walter Harding. Boston: Houghton Mifflin, 1995.

———. *A Week on the Concord and Merrimack Rivers*. With an introduction by John McPhee. Princeton, N.J.: Princeton University Press, 2004.

———. *Wild Apples*. Bedford, Mass.: Applewood Books; Chester, Conn.: Distributed by Globe Pequot Press, 1992.

Warren, Robert Penn. *John Brown: The Making of a Martyr*. Nashville: J. S. Sanders, 1993.

Wheeler, Ruth R. *Concord: Climate for Freedom*. Concord, Mass.: Concord Museum, 2000.

Wineapple, Brenda. *Hawthorne: A Life*. New York: Knopf, 2003.

INDEX